# In Earshot of Water

# Sightline Books

*The Iowa Series in Literary Nonfiction*

Patricia Hampl & Carl H. Klaus, series editors

# Paul Lindholdt

# In Earshot
# of Water

*Notes from the Columbia Plateau*

University of Iowa Press    Iowa City

University of Iowa Press, Iowa City 52242
Copyright © 2011 by the University of Iowa Press
www.uiowapress.org
Printed in the United States of America
Text design by Richard Hendel

The University of Iowa Press is a member of
Green Press Initiative and is committed to
preserving natural resources.

Printed on acid-free paper

Library of Congress Cataloging-in-Publication Data
Lindholdt, Paul J.
In earshot of water: notes from the Columbia Plateau /
by Paul Lindholdt.
    p.   cm.—(Sightline books)
ISBN-13: 978-1-58729-984-1 (pbk.)
ISBN-10: 1-58729-984-4 (pbk.)
ISBN-13: 978-1-58729-985-8 (e-book)
ISBN-10: 1-58729-985-2 (e-book)
    1. Lindholdt, Paul J.—Travel—Northwest, Pacific.
    2. Northwest, Pacific—Description and travel.
    3. Natural history—Northwest, Pacific.
    4. Human ecology—Northwest, Pacific.
    5. Northwest, Pacific—Biography.    I. Title.

F852.3.L56 2011
979.5—dc22
                                        2010037425

# Contents

# Introduction

*I do not know which to prefer,*
*The beauty of inflections*
*Or the beauty of innuendoes,*
*The blackbird whistling*
*Or just after.*
——WALLACE STEVENS

Sounds were the stuff of imagination for me as a child, the textures of a life that might be well or poorly lived depending on one's aural fortune. And so I have always found my breathing space within earshot of water, whether in the Seattle suburb where I came of age, on Vashon Island in Puget Sound, or in the arid inland Northwest where I live now.

There was a pond, its water muddy and calm. No surface water fed it. No stream bled it into Walker Creek or drained it to salt water. Its lifeblood flowed in an aquifer beneath the ground. Home builders dumped fill dirt to make foundations for houses nearby, my family's house included; they poured concrete foundations, driveways, patios, and walks. The rich hydrology of that low spot in soggy western Washington found outlet where it could. A seep of a pool in the bog welled up. Willows flourished, their slivers of leaves electric in the spring and summer, their thin red bark luminous in the winter and fall.

Beside that pond I liked to crouch in all four seasons, amid those leaves I climbed. Mud in the process of drying, I learned, makes a murmur as moist as the noise of parting lips in the thick of kissing. Raindrops striking the surface of a pond sometimes bounce first, as if indecisive, but one must hug the mud to see such a feat. Within the murky subtlety of that water I planted catfish, netted tadpoles and dragonflies, and watched winging swallows with their mouths wide open skim the surface to snap up scudding bugs.

Such memories continue to bubble up, especially now that I live in a strikingly different part of Washington. My bioregion lies at the edge of three ecotones — transitional areas between adjacent ecological communities.

To the north and the east, the topography rises and yields to stands of massive conifers, staggering canyons, muscular rivers and mountains, enormous lakes named Priest, Pend Oreille, and Coeur d'Alene. To the south ranges the milder Palouse, one of the planet's most productive wheat-growing regions, with its steep rolling hills and deep, rich volcanic loess soil. To the west lie channeled scablands and shrub-steppe desert, relieved in places by potholes and seep lakes. The word *channeled* recalls the remnant paths of prehistoric floods that coursed across the volcanic basalt rock and took the topsoil with it to the coast. The phrase *shrub-steppe* identifies the scab-rock basalt lowlands and treeless scrub brush threaded by badger burrows, rodents, and reptiles.

These regions include parts of both northern Idaho and eastern Washington. The entire geographical spread has gained a political identity known as the "Inland Empire" — a name that makes me fidget for its hints of "Manifest Destiny" and old imperialism. At one time this region depended for its stability on natural resources — timber, mining, ranching, agriculture, and traditional fishing by Indian tribes.

But extracting those resources forever is neither possible nor wise, because they are limited. The latest culture war, since the Pacific Northwest spotted owl battle of the 1990s, concerns flagging salmon species in the Snake and Columbia rivers. This battle is an intimate aspect of my place. Dams erected from the 1930s through the 1970s have come to function less as flood control and irrigation than as ports, hundreds of miles inland, for barging crops and tree fiber. Indian tribes enjoy legal standing to restore the fish, but those Spokane, Kalispel, and Coeur d'Alene people are holding back; they share a history of being treated unfairly in the courts.

Just as unsustainable are the eroding farm fields, the soil reservoirs that are failing due to chemical inputs and other efforts to boost short-term earnings. Tons of precious topsoil blow and flow to parts unknown. This part of the world now is coming to rely more upon recreation, tourism, and manufacturing than on natural resources. When natural resources dwindle, quality of life erodes, and the nature-based resources become more precious than jobs or gold.

One trait of these western provinces has been a reprieve from social obligations, a respite from moral codes. Many people here will not be told what to do, including those "people" known under U.S. law as corporations. Huckleberry Finn aims to head for the hills at the end of Mark Twain's novel. "But I reckon I got to light out for the territory ahead of the rest," Huck says, "because Aunt Sally she's going to adopt me and sivilize me, and I can't stand it. I been there before." Some of my neighbors, as if honeying up to Huck on his Mississippi River raft, are just as prone to mobility and itchy feet, every bit as skittish. Accountability to others and to place is difficult to champion when so many forces have lined up against it. Residents of the inland Northwest do not care for others telling them how to live, especially if those others represent the government. Their resistance to authority is an aspect of the place I write about.

Once I moved to this place in the inland West, I needed to answer to friends in the Seattle area where I came of age. Some wondered why I left the coastal corridor and its abundant water. The truth is, my father fostered in me a taste for "the big outside," a hunger that the arid inland West can best assuage. And so I lit out for the territories. Now that I have found my way, I aim to stay.

These essays, then, are a collective sigh for the trials and less evident pleasures of living in the rural Pacific Northwest. I left behind the temperate climes and the political liberalism of western Washington where I was born. I chose a rustic region, and that choice has made all the difference. It has its challenges, and I confess I sometimes wish I still were singing in the choir whose voices echo around Puget Sound and make Washington a blue state. Still, the trade-offs in wild nature just beyond my doorway make the sacrifice worthwhile.

# High Country

utside the town of Salmon, the Idaho high country stunts most growth. Buds of lupine and paintbrush, penstemon and pines, even the paddling mallard ducks grow tiny.

Late one day in May, songbirds had yet to lay their eggs, and winds still agitated Williams Lake—harsh habitat for creatures that adapt somehow and even thrive. Fat rainbow trout spawned or lunged for flies. Mule deer, their coats the color of basalt rock, clambered the sides of scab-rock canyons.

Near the mouth of a stream that flows from the lake, my father (Harold) and I had set up camp. Harold was tossing cracked corn to chipmunks and marmots. He fed them until they were stuffed and drowsy. He liked to watch animals eat. Already, at 4:00 PM, he had folded down his cot from the wall of the travel van we'd driven in. From the block of ice we bought in Salmon to keep food cold, he'd chipped some chunks that swirled in his bourbon.

I wandered down along the stream to its delta at the lake. In the vigorous water, amid fist-sized stones, a water ouzel or American dipper was searching for food. Bluebill ducks flashed past on the water, pursuing and eluding would-be mates.

Six months before, in Seattle, Harold had been told he had a prostate cancer so advanced that the doctor could see no alternative but to remove Harold's testicles, a procedure termed an orchiectomy. Harold thanked the oncologist, believing he had saved his life—my father, who liked to boast he had never been in a hospital, never taken an aspirin or suffered an illness. After I got his news in Idaho, where I was living at the time, my groin ached for days.

Williams Lake, deep and cold, is one of the few waters in Idaho that still supports healthy numbers of native trout. They swim from the lake each year to spawn, nosing north toward gravel beds on federal lands in Lemhi County. At the opposite end of the lake, vacation homes line the shore, half of them displaying "For Sale" signs. Their sewage — dishwashing detergents and human waste — flows into the lake and causes eutrophication, which is oxygen loss due to nutrient loading.

Eutrophication — the dizzy demand for oxygen placed on plant growth by aquatic ecologies — strangles streams and lakes. It occurs when sewage seeps from drain fields in residential areas, or when cow manure or fertilizers from croplands cause a bloom. Biology students in their laboratories learn early that bacteria in a Petri dish will expire from their own wastes.

What kind of a son was I to concern myself with water quality when my father was burning up with cancer? Harold, I reminded myself, taught me to fight for fish and birds and ecosystems. He sparked my interest in hunting and fishing, sports he gave up in later years. He taught me the importance of keeping public lands public. What caused his bloom of cancer cells, we will never learn.

On Williams Lake, fishermen cast bait from boats and banks. The most successful hauled home stringers and creels heavy with native rainbow trout, the orange flesh bright and firm. The fishermen wanted their luck to last forever, just as immigrants and Indians hoped the salmon that ran by the millions in the Snake River and the Salmon River would never fall away.

At eight years of age I had the sudden realization I was apt to outlive my father. I would have to undergo his death. I was scared and angry over that injustice. Like the blustery poet in Wales I wanted to cry out, "Do not go gentle into that good night!" A couple of times I even tried to pray I would go first, a selfish impulse to die before he did, if only to avoid the grief of loss.

On our last day in the camp, we drove the van atop a rimrock ridge to get a new view of the land. Lakes and rock and sage lay all before us. We were feeling a bit dispirited that our vacation was coming to an end. As we were saying goodbye to the place, a jet bomber bellowed past, almost at eye level, drowning the calls of chickadees and setting our teeth on edge. The blast sounded loud enough to fell a fir tree, alien enough to make a cow elk lose her calf. Ten miles from town, dozens from any military base, the ground beneath the feet of every creature trembled, and the air that buoys the birds gave way.

Some Indians say the highest honor to be paid to the dead is to carry on their work. That's what I resolved to do for Harold— complete some of the conservation labor he started so long ago. But I am worried about this land. So many of us view the planet as a simple steppingstone to heaven, a phase of life to be endured and overcome, like some protracted battle against unknown forces, or a run of rotten luck.

# Walker Creek

At the airport outside Seattle my family greets me — dogs and sisters, kids and Mom — everyone except our father, who has died of cancer two months before. My mother now looks shorter, my sister more brittle and thin, and the gaggle of nephews too timid and shy to meet my eye. We adults trade compliments and hugs.

Just moments and we're home, as the sisters and I still call it, a low ranch house surrounded by flowers and grasses and trees. We are in a suburb of Seattle, where ranchettes of several acres slope from the road to marshes and fields. Back to my youth I slide, to the garden overgrown in pumpkins we siblings planted, weeded, picked, and sold from the card table at the roadside; back to the grease pencils for marking pumpkin prices and the muffin tins for making change.

The acreage conjures up the abundant pets of my childhood, the herds and ponds and flocks. Once more I smell lanolin from lambs-wool on my hands and hear our beef cattle bawling for someone to toss them hay. Dazed by these memories and the summer sun, I wander out past tufts of orchard grass and blackberry canes, beside the weathered barn and sheds, to the busy willows grown from shoots that Harold and I cut and thrust into the soil.

I have flown back to help my mother in this difficult time but also to rendezvous with my son Braden, who is almost a man now. He and I will cultivate native shrubs and trees, haul bark and pull weeds, and try to finish the indigenous botany job my father began before he fell ill. In a vacant lot beside the house, he built an arching trellis over double benches that serve as entry to the would-be garden that lies beyond. Here we will do our spadework.

The garden has good drainage and southern exposure, a sweet setting in this region of fog and drizzle, whereas northern is dark and damp. Finding a place where native plants still grow in a spot that hasn't been grazed, bulldozed, drained, or sprayed is rare. The garden plot lies in the shade of a dozen Douglas-firs that Harold allowed to continue towering when he cleared the sloping lowland to the east for pasture—for horses, Hereford cattle, and sheep.

Nearly a century old, the firs have withstood roads and homes, phone wires and sewer lines, gas mains and power poles—even two stout bars embedded in their trunks for us kids to practice gymnastic stunts. When gales tried to topple the trees, we feared they'd fall on the house, but they still stand. We lopped their boughs to make Christmas wreaths and mantle mangers, flung ropes over the branches to fashion tire swings, and watched robins and orioles and blackbirds brood among their needles. We liked to think we used those old trees well. The grove was our evergreen sanctuary, the remnant wild space into which we gazed and wondered how it might prove useful.

On this visit to the family homestead I get reacquainted with the trees, marveling at the thick resilient bark, the pitch that smears my hands. The trees call up more than memories for me. They remind me that I have become what some would call a tree-hugger, a pantheist engaged in the praise of Earth's creations. Before I sit down to supper with my mother this evening, I will scrub with a hand brush to remove the sticky residue of those trees.

In the tribal way of those sustained by memories and blood, my family mostly lives near regular jobs and haunts, hanging on to early farmland turned suburbia. Anchor-hold for the kinfolk, the neighborhood is changing. People move in and out more often. Where we used to have sledding parties and borrow baking supplies, we no longer know who lives next door, much less several houses down. Exotic faces blend and blur with the freeway spurs, the quickie marts, the airport grown from one runway to three, the jets that take off so much closer now. Pollution, germs, and crime preoccupy my family's time and conversations. Homes burglarized in the daylight, automobiles hot-wired and stolen. The guard dog's yelping after nightfall prompts alarm.

Idling in traffic or shopping in town, I wallow in a haze of nostalgia, memories as thick and sweet as the scent of honeysuckle that cloys the yard in August and needs offshore breezes to disperse it. At other times the haze of the past seems like a vapor made tangible by auto exhaust and spent jet fuel, the odors that industrialists tell me smell like money. But I don't work in industry any longer, and haven't for years. I don't live here. If I yearn for the past, maybe it's my former self I yearn for, the one who tunneled through foxtail barley, crushed bracken ferns and nettles to make tunnels fit for hands and knees, who made plaster casts of raccoon tracks and captured garter snakes.

Heads and antlers of elk and deer jut from the indoor walls of my childhood home. So do the rifles and shotguns that used to be my diversion. The parquet pattern of teakwood floors, the corkboard walls that deaden sound, the cedar-sided house where I was born and raised—everything about this family landscape constitutes a kind of documentation I will try to read in the months I have to visit. There are my teeth marks on the maple chair I scraped in a petulant mood, there the garage where dragonflies from the marsh entered and got trapped, where they thrashed against the picture window, rested awhile and thrashed again.

In 1951 my father bought the land. It came with a swamp that sheltered ducks, geese, coyotes, and deer. Early settlers, to drain the swamp and make it suitable for grazing, dug a system of ditches that required constant clearing so the water would flow. Those ditches clog now with decaying cattails, willow leaves, fireweed and ferns, demonstrating the will of every swamp to die the slow and natural death that follows from accumulated tons of vegetation. The boggy marsh is classed now as a wetland, protected by state and federal laws and regulations, a portion of incorporated Burien, a suburb of Seattle. It has always been the headwater of tiny Walker Creek.

The swamp was dying a natural death until engineers built a freeway spur beside it. The freeway altered the hydrology so much that the swamp began again to brim with runoff water. One enterprising neighbor, his eye trained on the main chance, trucked in fill dirt to this wetland, planning to sprout rows of houses there. He never got the permits from the city, but the springs that give rise to the creek are entombed now by truckloads of concrete, blacktop, even by a set of wooden stairs that lie cockeyed, as if ill at ease. Today the swamp is little more than a sump for the freeway, airport, and nearby housing sites.

Where waterfowl used to breed, brackish runoff from the freeway spawns a colorful sludge. Some mallard ducks, urged by instinct against all odds, nest near the hidden springs of Walker Creek. In late July, when the standing water becomes so rank it hatches flies, the mallard hens try to guide their waddling broods to flowing water several blocks away. Some of the hatchlings end up grabbed by cats or flattened by cars on Des Moines Memorial Drive — so named for the veterans who fell during World War I.

Just south beyond the freeway sump, Walker Creek begins in earnest. To follow its first trickles to Puget Sound a half-mile away, you would need to tunnel under aquatic vegetation that looks firm enough to walk on. Suspended only by water, though, the plant mats would sink at once beneath your weight.

The water gurgles between and beneath the rushes and cattails whose sharp thin leaves divined the watercourse. Their genetic materials foretold the spring, even when they glimmered only as seeds embedded in guano between the toes of migratory swallows. The strong pliant stalks support redwing blackbird nests. When people in the Middle Ages saw a cattail swaying in the wind, they recognized it as a "reed mace." They saw in its shape a bog-grown weapon that was wielded for millennia by mortal gods who fought for power.

Cattails divine a water source — whether stream or marsh or desert pond. The willow wand of the water witch, whose work I witnessed when I was twelve, divined the aquifer in the Seattle suburb where I had my home.

Property developer Dick Shoemaker wanted to find the spot to drill a well when he built a new office park. To get it done, he hired the witch or diviner to dowse the knoll and locate where the well should go. With his red nose and squinting eyes, the alcoholic dowser in no way matched my vision of what a wonder-worker ought to be. His perceptive hands looked just like mine, and his shirttail trailed from droopy dungarees. On a low grass knoll textured by hawthorns and vine maples, he surveyed the land's contour. He squinted at the distance and spit. He lifted his chin, as if sniffing out a well-mixed drink. And then he crept across the knoll, halting here and there, stomping his feet, stopping, cocking his head like a robin listening for worms. He was foraging for just the proper clunk.

Satisfied at last with his location, he stalked to the swamp below the knoll and cut a forking crotch from a Pacific willow (*Salix lasian-*

*dra*), a shrubby member of that family of water-loving trees whose roots colonize septic tanks and water mains. From the willow he cut a long wand shaped like a slingshot. He gripped the wand by its twin ends, as one might handle plow traces or bridle reins. He walked as if he were plowing the land, his close-set eyes fixed so fine upon the willow crotch they almost crossed.

The wand wavered and hovered above the ground. It quivered and it twitched. Walking with greater care and slowing down, he waited, concentrated, for the forked stick to dip. With a downward yank it marked the spot. Contented, he licked his lips and wiped his sweating hands.

The backhoe came on a flatbed truck the next week. It slogged to the spot and clawed through fourteen feet of loam and clay. I spent two days digging farther, laboring for ninety cents an hour with a friend up top who pulleyed the dirt to the surface, both of us glad to have the work. Our boss said to keep on digging until we heard a hollow sound like a melon. Nineteen feet below the earth's crust, water rose to pool around my shoes.

South of my family's acreage, among roots of alders and poplars and willows, Walker Creek is sourcing still, the liquid surfacing invisible at first, at last a legible trickle inches deep and one foot wide. The water purls. It sends up notes like early music. It quickens the willows and grass. You are within earshot of water. Small trout hatched there and finning to Puget Sound might spook soon. Their dark backs will split the surface as they flash away. The earth is so spongy they do not need to see you. Vibes from your softest steps suffice.

The stream gathers force in the boggy acres worked by Mike and Irma Mortenson, siblings who shared a house on the hill across the highway. For many decades their family held the land. They admired it for the apple trees that gave good fruit without any sprays. The first time we met, I got busted picking apples from their trees. Irma hollered from her front porch, "Hey! What do you think you're doing?" I hung my head and walked her way.

Irma's father had built a slaughterhouse there. After her brother died, the zoning around her changed from residential to multiple, and Irma could no longer afford the taxes. The chores became too much and she moved into an apartment complex erected behind her Victorian home. She was just another being that got toppled by the undertow from a booming wave in real estate.

Once they leave the former Mortenson plantation, those trickles from bubbling springs have become the two-foot-wide north fork of Walker Creek. The water is clear, filtered and renewed by seeping through thick foliage in the valley bottom. Here salmon used to twitch upstream to spawn, in trickles and ditches so shallow that their bellies dragged with milt or egg sacs.

The ditches dug to drain the marshes and make pastureland baffled spawning fish. Eagles and ospreys congregated on creeks and salt shores each fall to feed on them. In his youth my father, Seattle-born, a first-generation Danish American, scooped up the salmon with porous burlap gunnysacks, sacks that served as weirs and kept the big fish damp until he got home. In my dreams I have walked those ditches with my boy-father. Under his guidance and his gaze, I have stumbled upon twenty-pound sea-run salmon floundering in the shallows of Walker Creek as if they had tumbled from the skies.

Below Mike and Irma's house, the family slaughterhouse drained into Walker Creek. The operation was planned that way, just as industrial factories have been situated for centuries, a story told more than a century ago by the Norwegian playwright Henrik Ibsen in his drama *An Enemy of the People.*

When a cocked sledge above a doorway fell, the skullcap cracked and the stunned beef blundered to its knees. A jockey hooked the jaw, jacked a handle, and raised the great weight upward until the rear hooves danced an artless jig on the slippery floor. Then a second laborer — a walking razor draped in a heavy apron — sliced and slipped the steer hide inside out. He stripped the heavy skin to the floor, transforming each Black Angus or red Hereford into the marbled white of its own fat. The steer carcasses must have appeared puzzled, blushing, wishing they were dressed. Water from Walker Creek, pumped in and out, flushed the building of its blood and ruptured bits.

Below the slaughterhouse site, Walker Creek crosses Des Moines Memorial Drive and skirts the yard of a bungalow home. When kids in that house were growing up, they stretched a net across the yard beside the water and fetched stray volleyballs from Walker Creek, yelping with delight.

But the kids grew up and left the nest, the house became mute, and wild beavers dammed the creek and flooded the yard. County officials destroyed the dam. The beavers rebuilt it. Persistent officials trapped the beavers and relocated them a dozen miles away. But the animals either padded their way back, or else another pair chose to carry on that earthy work, because a third dam began to take shape under the wrap of darkness. That was when the landowners called a halt to all the vain attempts at beaver control. The animals, they said, should be allowed to stay. Now the yard lies beneath the only beaver pond inside Burien city limits.

The beaver pond offers a welcome illusion that nature is reclaiming the land. Maybe Harold hoped to achieve the same illusion by planting his native garden. In a certain sense he was restoring the old pasture, handing it back to the very vegetation that had greened the source of Walker Creek before him.

An arching trellis above twin benches gives entry to the plot he began to plant. On the benches Braden and I rest between bouts of pulling weeds, pruning limbs, carting bark, and rooting plants. Braden kneels beside me as we work. It's as if we can see Harold hauling seedlings and bark and sweating. It is as if we're working side by side with him in the last of his earthly chores.

Leaves of clematis overspread the trellis and furnish heavy shade. Past the entry on the left, a pussy willow cascades. On the right a hawthorn scatters its white petals each spring, its fleshy crimson berries each fall. I use the hawthorn to give Braden his first lesson in how to prune the branches of a tree. Thin-skinned madrone, evergreen broadleafs whose papery red bark peels all year, volunteer from bird dung and curl toward the sun. Fir stumps nurse redcedar saplings. In the moist undergrowth creep salal and Oregon grape, queen's cup and bunchgrasses, false hellebore and kinnikinnick.

The arching trellis Harold built in this garden frames a leafy world that leans toward sunlight. It soothes its human viewers by growing green and clean. Weary eyes gain rest and sanctuary here. The shadowing firs bend from the west. Beyond the garden plot's confines, downhill and to the east, the aging swamp blooms and decays. South of the garden, Walker Creek gurgles in the ear of anyone who pauses to hear. It rehearses songs of birds and weeds and beavers, of salmon that swam in water so shallow they might have been breathing air. Eight minutes north as a mallard hen wings it, the city named for a wise Indian lies. Sleep would come easy in this spot, solace amid the bird songs and pollen, were not the nearby freeway and the airport jets so loud.

# Black Bear on Gold Hill

Along the Little Naches River in the Washington Cascades, my little boys and I were fishing for the cutthroat trout that dimpled the surface. It was early June, the wasps and mosquitoes few, summer's cauldron not yet scalding.

Beside that river a driver had gotten his big truck stuck. His spinning tires left a gouge where water collected. In the truck-tire puddle, a salamander larva floated, a "mud puppy" as I had heard my father term it, a creature that resembled an extinct Dimetrodon, chamois orange on its belly, dusky brown above. Fantastic gills protruded from its neckline, a stiff Elizabethan collar.

My boys dropped their fishing rods and crept to the puddle's edge. In that high mountain water the creature hung, suspended between the bottom muck and surface slime. It resembled a relic encased in ancient amber, a crystal solidified from salts, a freak of a child whose swimming skills had failed it when it tried the dead-man float. The kids gave a collective shudder.

Chase wanted to toss a rock, to make a splash, to bring it within reach. "Find a bug and try to feed it," I said instead. "Yeah!" they chorused, and the scrambling after grubs and worms beneath logs and stones began. I let out a breath, lounged against a tree, whistled some old tune and watched. Insects twinkled in the sun's late slant. Petals of Indian paintbrush darkly flamed. The purple firs across the river began to merge with their own shadows.

The arrival of this salamander, as E. B. White wrote of a dragonfly in Maine, "convinced me beyond any doubt that everything was as it always had been, that the years were a mirage and there had been no years." In this same alpine meadow, my father and one of his friends had shot with their pistols into a puddle much like this one. They had aimed for the salamander larvae. They had fired and fired again, delighting like boys when the splash and spray came, squinting as the water deflected the bullets. Their slugs drove through the shallow pond. They flung bubbles underwater and sent up plumes of silt.

I remember, too, that whisky fumes had mingled with the gun smoke. On the hills above the puddle, torn earth showed black from impromptu hill climbs on motorcycles and races over ruts. The men had taken turns on the dirt bike, ripping raw the meadow and the hills. Fourteen years old, wild about internal combustion, I had revved that motorcycle right along with them. But that was in another lifetime, and now both men are dead.

On a quieter trip to that same campground on the Little Naches River, my father and I had driven in late one night and roused a resting herd of elk that bedded in the meadow. The bulls rose first, wide-legged, and faced us. In our glare their eyes reflected back our shining like shook foil. When they all had thundered into the trees, I leapt from the truck and ran to the place where they had lain. The air hung heavy with the musk that lingered there. I palmed the meadow grass the elk had matted down then lifted it to my face to sniff.

By this time my children had trapped bugs in a cup and were pitching them to the salamander, which had yet to move from the aqua incognita, the middle ground between the muck and slime. Dusk already was making it hard to see. Time to gather up our fishing gear and thread a path through the meadow back to camp. There was food in the ice chest cooked and ready to eat.

As we left the newt behind, I thought to share some photographs I had brought along, dozens of snaps of my father, whom they had never met. A couple of the photos, I said to build suspense, came from this campground.

Back at camp we spread the album beneath a propane lantern's glow. Both boys sharpened elbows to crowd in close. Adhesive tabs held corners of the photos as if in frames. By bending the photo edges, we could slip them from the tabs, pass them hand to hand, and examine the inscriptions in a cursive hand on back. The first photo showed five men slouched in front of a cabin, hats dipped, hiding their eyes, pistols sloping from holsters; it bore no words, but I recognized my father, Harold, as the tallest of the bunch. The men looked like bandits crept from a hole in the ground who hoped their trail from the crime scene had gone cold. Another photo showed my father about the same age, in his twenties, bare-chested, lean, a rifle upended on a cocked thigh. Windy Ridge rose behind him, a gnarled conifer in the foreground.

I had not seen these photos in decades, and a pair of them surprised and bruised me. Before the boys could notice, I plucked them from the page and pocketed them for the rest of the camping trip. Both photos showed dead deer being goaded by men in a hunting camp. One photo displayed a doe clad in a woman's frilly panties and hoisted on her hind legs as if to dance with her red-and-black-plaid male mate. In another, a man on all fours was inserting a rifle barrel in the ass end of the cavity where the guts of the deer once lay.

Many of the snaps featured hunting trips, and the boys wanted to hear stories. I told them I had carried a shotgun on early outings, and had learned to lead a flying bird and stage the trigger-squeeze. They wanted more. And so I held out to them the story of my first bear hunt. Reed could chew a pensive cud as he heard about my venture. He had shown a recent interest in hunting, he had been practicing with his bow, and his mother promised him he could pursue whatever sort of game he chose, even if his choosing winged her heart.

When I was sixteen, I told the boys in the dark tent, I wanted to hunt big game. I grew up around guns, shot a lot at an early age, and enrolled in a firearm safety training course at twelve — a confirmation into the world of men, if one were to equate male maturation with such sacraments of the flesh.

Bear season opened in September, deer in October, and elk in November. For such big game I had a .30-30 Winchester carbine, the same lever-action weapon wielded by *The Rifleman* on TV. It was a good brush gun, which meant that twigs and leaves would be less apt to deflect its slow, heavy bullet than they would a faster, lighter lead sent from a longer barrel at a greater range. My father had given me the carbine. If I acquitted myself well with it, I would qualify for his .300 Weatherby, a rifle whose formidable knockdown power made me worry it would slam me senseless when it fired.

The Pacific Crest Trail, that international route connecting British Columbia with Mexico, bisected Gold Hill. Harold planned for us to car-camp just off Highway 410 near Chinook Pass. On opening day we'd hike the series of switchbacks to the trail up top. He had hunted Gold Hill and knew where the berries grew. Black bears feed on them in the fall to put on fat, raking fruit and leaves from low shrubs into maws that look much like a dog's. From the start of my project as a bear hunter, I had to face the irritation that my shorthair pointer reminded me of a bear, even ate berries off shrubs like one.

Harold and I set off up the hill before dawn. He was fifty years old, lean and fit, able to walk farther and faster than me on his worst days, and taller by five inches, a superiority he would always maintain. We both carried rifles, but his Weatherby had a variable scope sight, ideal for shots taken across vast voids.

We breakfasted on wild berries along the way. It was a good year, the fruit large and plentiful — the same fruit that people in the northern Rockies know as huckleberries. My hands and mouth were stained purple like a clown's when we crested the ridge and faced the east.

As I got into my tale, Chase began to rasp in his sleep. Wearied more easily than Reed, he required an extra hour of sleep every night. We had run him hard, his big-dog brother and I. Reed now was awake, though, fascinated by all my talk of ballistics and calibers and recoil pads. He broke into the story to ask if I had packed any of the guns Harold had left me. "Sorry," I said, "we couldn't shoot them in this campground even if we had them along. We'd get arrested."

When we hit the Pacific Crest Trail, my father and I headed north. The evergreens thinned and the view opened up. From someplace near, a dusky grouse clucked, tempting me to abandon bears and chase that witless wild chicken. Deep shade bathed the treetops across the valley, the exposure of that slope westerly, the altitude where we were hiking almost a mile high. Like a river meandering through a valley, the trail made its way along paths of least resistance. Tufts of wiry beargrass studded the sides of the trail, their white plumes long past fluffy prime, the remnant petals on the stiff stalks resembling messy feathers. The forest was a mix of spruce and subalpine fir, few of the trees more than thirty feet high at six thousand feet.

My father paused to sweep the binoculars over the frost-covered slope across the ravine. There the berries would be prime. The combination of chill mornings and hot afternoons created ideal conditions for wild fruit on those west-facing slopes. A gray jay squawked, though nowhere near us. It soared from tree to tree, followed by another. The birds were not sounding an alarm, just being vocal, as all jay species are. Our presence would remain a secret.

Harold exhaled and lowered the glasses, lowering his own silhouette as he did. *Across the canyon and below us, at least five hundred yards away,* he whispered, *a bear was feeding.* He handed me the binoculars and pointed. I strained, scanned, and within ten seconds the bear materialized from patches of shadows its same color. Head down, butt toward us, grazing like a cow. He asked me to take it, and told me the way to go. I would stalk by bushwhacking downhill to get close enough for a shot. In excited sibilants, he mapped the route. Then he put his .300 Weatherby in my hands. The distance I would need to shoot would be too great for my short brush gun with its open sights.

With a bout of pneumonia four years behind me, I had grown strong if not stout, and the gun was little burden. Nonetheless I respected its recoil enough to check the safety before I set off down the slope. Between the walnut stock and the leather sling I threaded my right arm. The barrel jutted upward behind my head. Bucking waist-high brush while trying to keep quiet, I angled toward the bear to bridge the distance between us and to get down to its same altitude for a straight shot across the ravine. Harold stayed behind and watched with the binoculars, leaving me the riflescope as my mechanical eye.

During the stalk I began to question my desire to become a hunter of big game. I slowed down. No outdoor folks rank bear meat high on their list of culinary pleasures. That recognition brought my manly ambitions into high relief: I was becoming a trophy hunter, something I had always despised. Worse, the bear was too far away to guess if its size would class it as a trophy, were I to aim for admittance to the Boone and Crockett Club, a society of shooters who have bagged the largest specimens of mammals on the planet.

Trophy hunting is counter-ecological, I already knew. It removes from gene pools the most magnificent animals that evolution has produced. Later in life I would lose sleep at the prospect that my species was apt to mount all the largest and grandest mammals in museums someday, or cache them on the walls of private homes. Those mammals left alive in their natural habitats would learn a stern genetic lesson to grow puny and unimpressive specimens only. A kind of reverse natural selection would take place, a survival of the plainest.

My thoughts were far less orderly as I slid the slope as softly as I could. I grabbed bushes to keep from falling; gouged heel-holds before stepping so as not to dislodge a rock, send it tumbling, and scare the bear. The labor of stalking made me pause to puff and contemplate greater labors if I were to nail it—the gutting and skinning, rolling up the heavy skin with hair, traipsing back to the truck to fetch a pack, quartering the animal, making trips up and down the switchback trail to tote those quarters back to camp. If I left the meat behind, there'd be larger loads of remorse to shoulder in later days, a waste of pain that would be solely my making. Hunters tend to agree that the body of a bear, stripped of its skin and paws, looks like nothing so much as a human nude.

By that time I was getting close enough for a shot. I could feel Harold's tense anticipation behind me, his glasses trained on the bear's backside, watching the animal pack on fat to last it through the winter.

To please my old man, I had turned from birds to big game— hoping to make him more proud of me, gain his attention and respect, give him a chest of stories. It was an ineffable guy thing. When I was ten, he had offered me a hundred dollars if I could beat him at arm wrestling, and six years later I still was loath to try. Not afraid to fail, I was instead unwilling to train to the task or try to rise to that contrived occasion. If I beat him, our relationship would change. If I trained to beat him, I would be capitulating to the same pressure that had enlisted me to take boxing lessons at the tender age of seven, my scrawny arms striking the face of the trainer at Gentlemen's Gym.

As I looked for a tree-fork to steady the rifle on, a great ambivalence gripped me. There was a chance I would only wound the bear, then have to follow its trail of blood and risk being waylaid as I tracked it, or face the likelihood it had crawled away to die. None of my alternatives seemed at last attractive. What was I doing? I wanted to Peter-Pan my own way through my teens, remain a purple-faced kid, sit down amid berry bushes and slurp the succulent fruit.

The crotch of one sapling fir tree was just the right height. I crouched and settled the scope on the animal some three hundred yards away. I would have to aim a little high to allow for the bullet-drop at such a distance. Just as I was manning up, readying myself to rebel against every rationale to be practical and compassionate, the sun crested the horizon and flooded the lens of my riflescope with light. A blinding radiance obliterated the crosshairs.

I lowered the gun. I fiddled with its safety lock for a few seconds, flicking it on and off, trying to decide what to do, what to say. Then I turned away, headed back, bucked brush loudly now, reckless with noise, my entire being made lighter by the lifting of my gutless doubt.

What if I had been too slow in the stalking? What if I had gamed the dawn unconsciously and kept my manly arrival at arm's length? I had a ready alibi for not having gotten the shot. Many humans go their whole lives without spilling blood, I knew, just as some humans die with their virginity intact, full of contentment perhaps. The hike back to camp would be much more pleasant without the heft of hair, skin, flesh, blood—and without the less tangible stuff that was certain to outlive a felt-trimmed rug or an open-mouthed head mount.

In the tent beside the Little Naches River, I turned to Reed to gauge his reaction. My story could not possibly have fulfilled him, I thought. He had clutched at every word, inserted himself into the scenes, almost tasted the berries and heard the rifle's overdue boom on that early September day. The tale I told wasn't gory; it wasn't even inclined to frighten. And yet he seemed more contented than I thought he would, when we said our goodnights. My son was learning to appreciate the complex trajectory of narrative's demands.

We stretched our full lengths out in our sleeping bags, story time over. He turned away from me and let out a deep sigh. In the light from the stars that the mesh canopy let through, I could just make out his slender shape.

# In the Shadow of the Government's Blind Eye

iking between the towns of Tukwila and Kent, not far from Seattle, I came upon a place where no grass grew, a scorched plat of land in Washington, the Evergreen State. Industrial rubbish lay in heaps there, and colossal tanks on stilt legs towered. Pheasants cackled from patches of blackberry briars. Pintail ducks drove wedges overhead, and dairy cattle lowed from flood-lush fields.

That scar upon the landscape rattled me for days. Its blacks and grays collided with clusters of native bunchgrass on its perimeter and clashed with the red of the rosehips, causing me to object aesthetically, in my teenage way. Not that I could smell anything. As a sight animal trained from youth to hunt and gather — marbles and pop bottles, rail spikes and mushrooms, pheasants, berries, trout — my susceptible vision overwhelmed my companion senses. Most mammals, more sensitive than we humans are, tune into the complexities of Earth through a refined olfactory capacity to sense chemicals.

And so my eyes despised the outsized tanks for storing fluids, the ponds of acids that teetered between liquid and gas, the makeshift foundry and its dusty heaps of fly ash, and the tangibly dangerous disorder. With its six-foot cyclone fence and rusty barbed wire, the Western Processing Company site might have been a compound for prisoners during World War II, a test plot for nuclear bombs, or the scorched aftermath of a widespread fire. I could smell none of its history, though. I could sniff nothing strictly astray. A year later I agreed to work in that place and discount the damning evidence of my own eyes.

Now, wearing shorts in the morning sun some decades later, I can see traces of the accident, corrugations on my thighs, scars where hair refuses to grow, marks like contour lines on a map. In good light they resemble stretch marks, vestiges of new growth, reminders of another size and time.

Once I graduated from high school in Seattle, I turned to blue-collar work, just as my father before me had done. I swung hammers, molded molten plastic, canned seafood, and drove forklifts. Adrift in industrial America, I learned how to tell myself stories to hide the truth about my family, region, and culture. Twelve years after I worked there, Western Processing became the largest Superfund site in the coastal Northwest, a landscape that inspired sophisticated engineering feats and required some seventy million dollars to try to restore. At about that same time, I became the first descendant in my paternal line to aspire to a higher education.

Away from the smokestacks and hardhats, I gravitated to libraries. In those sanctuaries I sniffed out whatever I could about Western Processing and its effluents, the Environmental Protection Agency's (EPA) recriminations and the company's denials, the corporate consent decrees and the extravagant cleanup costs. I needed to find how far I'd compromised my bioregion and my health. The technical brochures of my continuing education, the newspaper stories, interviews, and visits with former coworkers, renovated my memories and impressed me with the brute force of American big industry and business.

Herb Gaskell began overseeing Superfund remediation at Western Processing when the Boeing Company bought the site in 1984. Over the phone, Herb sounded keen to talk when he learned I had worked there ten years earlier. He invited me to tour the former factory grounds.

Nature and industry appear to purr in harmony at the site today, a testimony to technical resourcefulness. Tidy roads, fences, dikes, grass, and gravel have transformed it into a location fit for picnicking and capering with the kids. But Herb himself seems much in need of serious intervention. He chain-smokes Chesterfield straights, and the gouged pouches beneath his bloodshot eyes make him seem hound-sorry to see his career conclude in such a way. "You'll need to put on this hardhat and goggles," he tells me between coughs. "EPA requires it."

Putting on the hardhat takes me back to 1974. The nylon riggings suspend my skull inside the yellow shell. I nod at Herb and knock my knuckles on the plastic noggin, which amplifies the hollow sound. Herb nods back. The goggles fog up once we get outdoors, though, and very soon we're gaping through a haze of condensation. Why the pretense of precaution after all these years, I wonder. I used to play patty-cake in far worse stuff than this.

My guide grows wary when I take out a notebook and begin to ask him questions. He has been through this routine before—writers sniffing for some toxic muck to rake. "Boeing is paying seventy-eight percent of the clean-up costs," he recites, "which so far have run sixty-seven million dollars. Two dozen other contributors and EPA are paying the rest." By *contributors*, I learn, Herb means other companies that agreed to pitch in and absorb part of the landscape-laundering expenses. A legally precise word, *contributors* suggests the costs are voluntary, as if no one were requiring them to pay.

From two hundred government and corporate customers, Western Processing accepted millions of gallons and thousands of tons of industrial byproducts. The soil beneath the site contains cadmium, cyanide, dioxins, phenols, and trichloroethylene. Surface cleanup sent twenty-five hundred truckloads of saturated soil to the town of Arlington in arid eastern Oregon—the dioxins alone so volatile that every commercial incinerator in the country "declined to accept the material for reasons of regulatory uncertainty and public resistance."

By declaring bankruptcy, Western Processing exempted itself from liability for the cleanup expenses. The owners or partners also cannot be held accountable under the provisions of U.S. corporate law.

Herb leads me up the stairs of an observation tower. At the top, we overlook the slabs of grass and the intentional ponds where mallard drakes paddle. A series of 206 wellheads, which join to three thousand feet of plumbing underground, jut from the ponds and grasses. We are seeing only the visible portions of an extraction well system meant to flood and filter the soil of its twenty-year accumulation of industrial wastes. Theoretically, water permeates and purifies the dirt. But where does the flushed and filtered fluid go? The wellheads themselves look like industrial-strength sprinklers.

"I have a chemical engineering degree," Herb acknowledges when I ask, "also an MBA from University of Washington, followed by my CPA. I've been with Boeing for seventeen years, done a variety of work." It occurs to me his preparation is ideal. His credentials bring together the convoluted chemistry and the complicated accounting necessary to do the tricky job.

Once our goggles are off and our heads unhatted, Herb lights up a fresh Chesterfield, leans back from his desk, and asks if I'd like to write a history of the site for hire. His offer takes me by surprise and my guard hackles rise. I need to think about it, I reply. Herb hands me two technical brochures, both issued by Boeing, about the cleanup project. I thank him and take my leave.

The brochures are remarkable bits of engineering. The writers worked hard to vanquish any recognition of the waste site's impact on the ecosystems or on attendant lives, human or otherwise. The task of cleaning up the site is broken down into several sets of rational objectives and goals to be achieved by means of the applied sciences.

Rather than acknowledging the site as a habitat where humans and other mammals lived, labored, ate, bled, and sloshed through toxic waters, the Boeing-generated brochures feature only factory laboratories. No faces show behind the helmets and the goggles.

The alliance of military and industrial interests at the site goes back some fifty years. That's when the Air Force utilized the angular wedge of land to harbor Nike missiles. Those anti-aircraft arms, stored in hidden silos underground, exemplified the greatness of military hardware during the Cold War. Behind a finger of Puget Sound, on nearby Vashon Island, a companion batch of Nike missiles was hidden in bunkers guarding against any incursion from the Pacific. The U.S. military had to build those bunkers close to Boeing, which remains a national hub for aerospace manufacturing and Pentagon contractors. Boeing commanded the market on protection technology.

A sort of reciprocal expansionism must have ensued. The intelligence and hardware of warfare that the area nurtured, even in times of relative peace, necessitated ever-greater hardware and software to guard it. The presence of sensitive equipment warranted further security measures. But what, besides the billions of involuntary tax dollars, did those tools truly cost to develop? Few numbers survive the historical record. Several monstrous drain pipes from the old Nike site at Western Processing poured into King County Drainage Ditch #1, which emptied finally into the Green River, in turn becoming the Duwamish River before discharging into Elliott Bay.

When I was coming of age in the 1960s, the Green River used to be good for steelhead, those seagoing rainbow trout that strobe up Pacific Northwest streams to spawn. During the long winters, just after dawn and before dusk, fishermen waited for steelhead to strike. As the years swept past, the strikes grew fewer. Steelhead numbers tumbled. The U.S. Fish and Wildlife Service tried to replace natives with hatchery-raised fingerlings, but they could not survive the lower river.

At its terminus in the bay, several miles downstream from the Western Processing site, the Duwamish River passes many factories before it dissipates within the chilly salt of Puget Sound. Few fishermen, even the most persistent Indians, now bother to try to gather anything from that river valley. Officials list its migratory fish runs under the Endangered Species Act.

The poet Richard Hugo, a native son of Seattle and one-time technical writer for Boeing, composed some early poems about the Duwamish River and the fish runs it supported. Hugo grew up in White Center, very near to the river, just up from steep Pigeon Hill. He grieved the changes taking over the Duwamish delta. As early as the 1960s, that delta had become a sluiceway for every factory and housing tract as far south and east as Black Diamond. In his books *A Run of Jacks* and *Duwamish Head*, Hugo trained a tragic eye on the hobos living in shacks along these banks, poor folks attached fast to the river as a stable presence in a swiftly shifting world. The last I heard, PCB levels were running so high in the Duwamish delta that hydrologists and government officials were cautioning fishing enthusiasts not to eat the sole or cod they caught with rod and reel. In his early fifties, in 1982, Richard Hugo died of cancer in Montana where he had moved to write and teach.

The Kent Valley that surrounds Western Processing once was flush with farms — some dairy, berry, or lamb operations — mostly of the family truck variety owned and run by citizens of Italian or Japanese descent, many of them Nisei or second-generation Japanese Americans. The farmers loaded fruits and vegetables into pickups and sold them from tailgates at roadside stands along the valley or at the Pike Place Market.

As a schoolboy I chased ducks and pheasants with my dog and shotgun along railroad tracks each fall, crashing my way through treacherous brambles and reed canary grass, into fields planted with squash, broccoli, or cauliflower that appeared somehow indigenous to the place. Now parking lots and warehouses, shrewdly called industrial parks—to soften their affront—throng the river valley.

The changes overtaking this area have become a kind of second nature. Everyone accepts and expects the concrete factory fronts and big-box stores. Everyone seems to need the products and the services those places offer. I call it a sacrifice region—once gorgeous, fertile, now gone to commerce. Clark Humphrey, writing for *The Seattle Weekly*, dubbed the region "Kent's vast miles of faceless, windowless warehousery and wide, sidewalkless arterials."

Soil in the valley was lush after centuries of flooding. The Green River always overflowed its banks and kept farms fresh by spreading organic matter from firs and alders and maple trees upstream. By 1958 the Army Corps of Engineers got busy solving the flooding dilemma with a system of earthen dikes that walled in the Green River and made big industry in the valley not only feasible, but sure.

More than industrial interests were at stake. Boeing, one of the largest Pentagon contractors in the nation, had located there. In the 1960s and 1970s the company dumped hazardous wastes at the Western Processing site. A Boeing attorney asserted in court that the site was "duly licensed and approved by the relevant environmental agencies."

This is my home, my birthplace and familial estate. My people often have urged me to return for visits from other states and counties, and I do. During those visits I hurry and wait in checkout lines or motor past the vast paved concrete warehouses. On occasions, the vertigo of blood's memory can startle me. With a start I might remember I used to play there as a child or hunt there as a young man, cut cattails, or romp there with my dog. Once I stooped to untangle a mat of cockle burrs from her ears on that very spot.

Western Processing founder Garmt Nieuwenhuis acquired the site in 1958 and began business by processing animal byproducts. Adopting technologies developed during World War II, Nieuwenhuis contracted to take wastes from slaughtering operations and turn a profit by converting them into commercial products. Horse hooves and cow horns became glue. Bones were ground into meal for fertilizer.

East of the Cascades the fertilizer market flourished, especially in the Columbia Basin, whose arid climate and meager topsoil made it ready for a postwar boom in chemically intensive agriculture. One of Nieuwenhuis's mainstay fertilizer products was zinc sulfate, a crude brew of zinc dross dissolved in sulfuric acid and suspended in water.

As the years passed, Nieuwenhuis found he could grow his company's profits more by recycling industrial fluids and tailings than by selling products outright. His best clients became military affiliates. The Puget Sound Naval Shipyard paid Nieuwenhuis to take away the corrosive wastes generated from electroplating nautical fittings and from cleaning hulls and holds. Boeing and Pacific Car and Foundry Company paid him to dispose of their enigmatic liquid refuse.

Much of it arrived on the factory grounds in tanker trucks and fifty-gallon drums. We laborers struggled to test, drain, store, neutralize, and dispose of those liquids. None of us had the training to perform such technical tasks. My partners were high-school dropouts, ex-convicts, drug-addled rock and rollers — often all three. We were the corrosive wastes of society that no one else was willing to take in. And that fact made us beholden, willing to put up with lots of grief. We rarely knew whose products we were handling, where they should go, or what was splashing on our heads and hands and feet.

The Green River region later grew infamous for a serial killer whose victims were found there, a murder case that took decades to solve. Most bodies were those of troubled runaways, would-be hookers, picked up on the motel strip near the SeaTac airport, chiefly racial minorities in their mid-teens. Speculation swirled that the perpetrator was a vigilante cop, a Green Beret, a man who knew the hangouts and had the skills to escape detection. In truth he was a factory hand. One of my high-school chums stepped on a corpse while fetching his remote-controlled airplane from bushes on a slope. The river, the bodies, and the factory intertwine in our collective memories today.

One day I scrawled a note upon a Space Needle postcard and sent it to a girlfriend far away. "Greetings from the city named after a wise Indian. I've been running every day and I feel strong. A vanity plate on a car read 'XCTABLE,' the driver grinning. A clinic at an inn tomorrow will show me how I can be wild and sensitive at the same time! What I'd do if I had wings. You say you wish I missed you more. What can I say or do? Jets from the nearby airport sound as though they're crashing in the yard and garden, and so I buy my water. The sky-blue empty carboy bottles ring like drums. Give me a gift and I might lose it. Give me yourself and you might lose it. Several miles away the Green River flows. When I was a child, restaurants used to sell syrupy sweet drinks by that name. Just another irony, I guess. But I'm out of space, gotta go. Remember that you're OK in my book."

A strange and estranged time and place. My high number in the lottery spared me a tour of Vietnam. From the jungles of that country my friends were coming home tweaked by PTSD, strung out on drugs, or never coming home at all. One smuggled a kilo of heroin back with him when he came, later dying in its clutches. Rock and roll music was battering our ears. Before our eyes the face of the landscape we had inherited was changing, human numbers booming, birds and fish dwindling, planes and rocket rumors screaming from the skies. Young women were being dumped along the river, murdered, and no one could learn why. Drugs by the boatload, heavy depressants, were hitting the streets from Asia, intensifying the oppression of gloomy weather and an ailing bioregion we called home.

News of a job opening at Western Processing came from Mike, a jolly heroin addict, an accidental friend. Both of his parents, heavy smokers who traveled to nearby Indian reservations to buy their cartons of Marlboros, died of cancer within two short years of one another when he was in his late teens. Mike had to find his way in the world. I befriended him when he kicked junk. How good of him to get me the job, I thought. The guys at the plant were OK, he assured me, and the commute a simple swoop along the valley highway.

Dopers around Seattle shunned the word *heroin* as though it were a curse. They said *junk* or *smack*, sometimes *horse*. Mike bounced from junk to meth and back again. When he decided to kick, he settled into an old rental house by the kindness of our friend Darryl Nelson. Mike kicked his habit in a closet cloistered from the rest of the house by a buffalo robe that fell across the door. Inside it, he lay groaning for days, grinding his bad teeth. The other tenants in the house could smell his telltale sweat. After his ordeal with heroin, he put on a blue collar and began to work for a living. Later, at twenty-five, he would require a set of dentures. He was my friend even though I knew "once a junkie always a junkie," which means beware, don't dare trust one.

Mike labored in the open-air foundry at Western Processing. The plant operated chemical and smelter divisions, and Mike labored to smelt waste zinc chunks into ingots. The shop had no walls, just a framework and a roof. From the high plateau of hindsight now, I see how that foundry resembled scenes from *Life in the Iron Mills*, the 1861 novella that focuses on Welsh immigrants in West Virginia. The zinc dross needed to be jack-hammered into pieces small enough to hurl into the furnace and melt.

The jack-hammering became a macho contest, the workers taking turns with Mike at the ear-splitting pneumatic tool, their bellies jiggling above its rough percussion, their faces fixed in frowns to show how hard they worked. At day's end, each one added up the tons he had sundered. A road of zinc cinders meandered across the acreage to the chemical section, where I earned my dollar-sixty an hour.

The author of *Iron Mills*, Rebecca Harding Davis, waxed sappy and romantic when she drew her character Wolfe. Awed by the ruling classes, Wolfe treats his family sweetly. In Davis's book, Wolfe gets a visit from a factory owner who stuns him into admiration. The poise and grace of his boss cause him to imagine God. "Then flashed before his vivid poetic sense the man [ . . . ] the pure face, the delicate, sinewy limbs, in harmony with all he knew of beauty or truth. In his cloudy fancy he had pictured a Something like this." The industrialist overlords seemed rarified and always out of reach. Wise and sensitive Wolfe, a good man who manages to endure the industrial work, yearns to give his ebbing energies to nurture his coworkers and family.

The laborers I knew, on the contrary, lashed their anguish back at others. One of my superiors at Western Processing, a bearded stooping Winston smoker by the name of John, got in my face one day, threatened to amputate my limbs and make a suitcase of my trunk — for an offense I now forget, for whatever imagined slight. I backed off from his blown-up bravado. If abused children forward abuse, frustrated factory workers carry fractured dignities and wield them like weapons above the heads of friends and spouses and kids. I saw that pain and desperation firsthand. I felt it grind me too.

The office where I met my boss was the second story of an unpainted building, shingle-sided and entered by ascending spindly stairs. When I rolled up in my panel truck, I took one look at the place and almost drove back home. As outlandish as it sounds, a puddle of water rounded the building, a pond that was a consequence of having no proper storm drains on the factory grounds. To get to the stairs in the fall and winter, one had to wade. I stubbed out my Kool Mild in rich disgust and shut the door of the truck with a thud.

The fleshy secretary, ever skeptical and unhappy on the job, was known as Mrs. Miller. She told me that Mr. Garmt Nieuwenhuis, my would-be boss, would see me in a moment. I peeped through his open door, spotted a small bald pate and a fringe of neat-trimmed gray, a Charlie Chaplin mustache, some rubber boots standing at attention beneath a grimace of window, and a military trench coat stippled with rain and flung across a chair.

"Yes?" He scowled and bounded toward me, never offering to shake hands. As I had been taught, though, I reached for and gripped his diminutive fist. I told him I had come to see about the job, that Mike had referred me. When I handed him a copy of my resume, he took it as one might take a hazardous laboratory specimen. He scowled again and slid it to his desk.

"You know how to drive a forklift?" he asked with a heavy Dutch accent. Without guile, I told him yes. Mike could give me lessons after hours.

"And what do you study in college?" he wondered aloud, approaching as if to discern some hidden knowledge inside my eyes. The truthful answer was that I had yet to declare a major but—here inspiration seized me—I said I was considering chemistry. For the first time the scowl vanished from his face. I felt as if I had connected. Later Nieuwenhuis would pay for my part-time college classes in exchange for my working at his factory forty hours a week. And for that long year I would become one of his willing functionaries.

Everyone at Western Processing wore boots. Rubber rain gear was de rigueur. At ten in the morning and three in the afternoon, when we broke for instant coffee and a smoke, day-shift laborers waded toward the office stairs. We waded everywhere around those flooded sixteen acres. Rain fell in sheets and drizzles and fogs. Rain pooled and blended with oil and diesel and zinc, splashing beneath our feet. In the steady twilight of those fall and winter days on the Washington coast, we never knew what we were wading through, never considered or cared. If we slipped and took a fall, if a valve or fitting broke while we were working with it, our rain gear served us as our sole protection. The nonunion company did not furnish us goggles or showers or gloves.

Western Processing profited from customers that generated wastes they could neither dump nor store within the law. Those wastes came loaded with heavy metals suspended in acids. Some of the acids had been used to etch electrical circuitry, others to bathe and sizzle jet plane components clean. We never really knew what they were; corporate disclosures were never required.

With forklifts we hauled fifty-gallon barrels lashed to pallets made of thin pine laths. A reckless tine of a forklift, an aim askew, pierced a drum and drained half its contents before it could be swung to the lip of a pond meant to hold it. In a warehouse with walls, such a spill would be a big enough mishap to evacuate the place. But the open yard of Western Processing allowed us to forget about it as soon as the laden liquid had finished draining to the dirt.

My partner in draining the drums was Ron, a wiry blond with sharp nose and chin. He devoured Camel Filters. Ron drove the lift to spear the pallet and hoist the drum to a draining place. I twisted a special wrench atop the drum to open it—one end of the wrench unthreading the vent, the other unplugging the bung. Ron then set the forklift's brake and climbed aboard the teetering pallet. Together we tilted the cumbersome four-hundred-pound drum, straining with danger and pain while its contents slopped to the pond and chugged to lighten our load.

Sometimes the drum would escape us and fall on its side, cracking the slats of the pallet board and glugging every which way. Sometimes a drum would plunge to the pond and send an enormous splash we'd scramble to avoid. Some drums that had escaped their handlers bobbed beyond anyone's reach or care. Others sank to be eaten by the acid.

The ponds stretched along one side of the long entry drive, each pond numbered, each harboring a unique mix of liquids. We constructed the ponds by bulldozing plots that measured seventy-five by one hundred fifty feet, and then piling layers of sawdust over a dirt floor. The dust we raised in laying the ponds was doubtful, because the site had been in operation for more than fifteen years. The complex stratifications at the site, once the Superfund cleanup began, proved marvelous for their collected chemical compounds.

While layering beds of sawdust to build a pond one summer day, I observed the toxicity and volatility of that saturated soil firsthand.

Preparing to light a cigarette, I could not believe my irritated eyes. Vaporous flames were playing across the sawdust bed I had patted flat. The flames appeared so light, like hummingbirds hovering above flowers, that I wasn't certain at first what I was seeing. The reaction was kind of sublime; the chemical sludge, that is, had turned into a gas. I scrambled away while my handiwork, the layer of sawdust I had laid, began to smoke and smolder below invisible flames.

The second stage to build the holding ponds involved transporting immense concrete tongue-in-groove blocks. Each weighed close to a ton and was fashioned by sinking a braided cable into the concrete form before the concrete hardened. We drove a chugging nine-ton Hyster forklift to skewer those braided cable bails, lift the blocks, and arrange them in a zippered line to form the perimeter of the pond. Then we spread a plastic liner across the sawdust base and up the sides of the interlocked blocks. We secured the liner atop each block with special concrete nails and slats of fragile lath.

The purpose behind the liners—huge expanses of plastic sheathing—was to confine toxic liquids. Liners still are promoted as the latest technology and used for landfills. Imagine digging a hole in your yard and draping a tarp inside the cavity to make a swimming pool; now fill that cavity with toxic wastes. Engineers of sanitary landfills (the current euphemism for garbage dumps) continue to promote liners for capturing the leachate that drains from garbage and taints the aquifers that recharge human drinking waters. Mineral engineers who design tailings ponds rely on the same kinds of immense industrial tarps to contain the cyanide waste used to liquefy gold in mine sites.

Tanker trucks that traveled to Western Processing emptied their liquid freight straight into the ponds from their hoses measuring four and six inches in diameter. The trouble was that the liners often leaked, requiring us laborers to find the leaks and try to patch them. That meant pumping the pond's contents back into tanks, draining the ponds, and then checking over the slimy liners.

In the meantime the region's rains were always falling, confounding our work and overflowing those ponds whose liners didn't leak. And so the toxic liquids meant to be recycled seeped instead beneath the ponds or saturated the soil. When we walked or drove the road, we splashed through sheets of flowing acid. Ever since those early slipshod recycling days, I have observed how many mining sites and factories, along with aluminum plants and pulp mills, have been sited without fail beside rivers, streams, lakes, and bays whose proximity allows them to flush their toxic wastes away as if by accident.

The liquids stored at Western Processing proved most dangerous if contained, and the open-air feature of the ponds helped to dissipate their volatility. Downwind, whenever a rare wind rose in the still Kent Valley, we workers could detect the gasses sublimating from the gleaming surfaces of the ponds. We could not smell them so much as we could taste them through our tongues and noses, sip them through the pores of our exposed faces and hands. Once I began to work at Western Processing, its lively electromagnetic environment began to speak to me on levels other than the visual.

Crossing a rusty catwalk one August day, leaning above a tremendous expanse of smoking hydrochloric acid, my eyes smarting, my head bathed in fumes, I could feel the threads of my life tighten and grow fine. I watched and saw small flocks of waterfowl circle, chuckle, and fall, their wings cupped, until they got close enough to flare away at the sight of the flakes of flame that shot above the surface, fires that ignited and died at the bidding of extraordinary powers, subject to no perceptible law. I grew dizzy from those heights, weary of all the prospects offered by life, and damned if I could understand why.

Like the fifty-five-gallon drums, the pumps we used to move liquids came strapped on pallet boards for easy transport. They were simple to wire and prime. Removing a carriage bolt atop the cylinder exposed a spongy filter where the priming fluid could be poured or any offending debris freed. One day, from inside the cylinder of a malfunctioning pump, a mass of black goo slid. It looked like leaves or grass or a wet black rag. It looked like anything but what it was — the decaying corpse of a western grebe.

That diving bird had lit in a pond holding oil rather than acid, and so it had not liquefied. Three of us laborers gathered and stared, then tossed the corpse over the chain-link fence. Stupid bird. Before I slogged back for some coffee, I could not help but guess how it had been for the grebe. Flustered by fog and far from its haunts on Puget Sound, lost in the vapor lights that flooded the roaring factory yard, it must have spotted the pond and landed there worn out. Unable to fly from the oil on its feathers, it starved.

One of my jobs involved neutralizing acids on a small scale, then putting those ratios into practice on the ground—literally, for the terms of our work required us to pump chemical slurries straight to the dirt. We tried to balance the signature pH, the percentage of hydrogen. The lower the pH, the more acidic; the higher the pH, the more caustic. A pH of seven, the acidity of water, became the target of our bumbling efforts to recycle the liquids we found in the ponds. Having hit that target, our bosses reasoned, those industrial wastes would be neutral enough to elude detection in the water.

Most ponds held acids whose stench and erratic tendency to burst into flames unsettled us. But the acids were less dreadful than the heavy metals they contained, the substances such as lead, now implicated in learning disorders and a range of neurological dysfunctions; mercury, known to cause blindness and hair loss; and other suspended metals apt to attack the human immune system. To be asked to pump such stuff into the soil became more at last than I could stand. The job was eating me alive by slow degrees.

From the company's own laboratory, I telephoned the EPA. It had just come into existence. The EPA only needed to be alerted, I felt sure, and they would make the nasty violations cease.

Come and look at this mess, I urged the disembodied voice on the phone. You don't need to enter the gates. Oil and acid has seeped past the fence and into surrounding ditches. It's visible from the dead-end road on the north, from the interurban trail that runs above it on the east where I had first seen it, and from the very air. Test the water in Mill Creek and see.

But my naive faith in the system occasioned no visits from EPA to my knowledge, no closures of the plant, no fines for mishandling the chemicals that we might as well have pumped directly to the creek. Boeing, whose nearby factories gave us so much business, probably could help explain the special government dispensation granted to the plant.

Western Processing was basking in the shadow of the government's blind eye, concealing itself in the deep shade created by the military-industrial complex, the unholy union that still perpetuates so much of the arms race today. We poor schmucks, undereducated and self-medicated, were meddling in chemicals we had neither the aptitude nor the savvy to handle—substances that needed to be managed with the utmost scientific care.

The factory's most oppressive chore involved the pumping of acid from a pond to a five-thousand-gallon tank, its liquid agitated by a custom paddle mounted above. We used that tank to neutralize the acid before we pumped it to the dirt. To make the process work, we shoveled powdered slack lime into the tank and produced slurries ranging in hue from a dull orange to Duwamish River brown. The job grew oppressive because it was hard work, grunt work, and it left ugly stains. Again I was responding aesthetically, but soon a sympathetic sense developed that extended me beyond appearances alone.

Dwayne and I shared that graveyard shift, from eleven at night to eight in the morning. Dwayne smoked Marlboros, whose filters were said to contain fiberglass that could render smokers sterile. Smoking them became a macho jeer in the face of fate, a fillip akin to dosing oneself with unknown drugs.

Dwayne wagged his head from side to side like a bear and turned his toes in when he walked. On graveyard shifts all of us got cranky, the more so if anyone had disturbed our sleep throughout the day. I showed off to Dwayne a sign I devised to tell friends and salespeople not to wake me. On the sign I sketched a gravedigger, a chump who looked like Oliver Hardy, spading high a mound of dirt. In place of the headstone, a sign within the sign cautioned all potential callers this way: "RIP. Gravedigger Sleeping. Do Not Disturb."

Dwayne and I had much to learn to operate the front-loader, a tractor with hydraulic bucket that scooped, tilted, fell, and rose. We learned on the job. Scoop the bucket full of powdered lime, drive the loader to the tank, raise the laden bucket to the tank's high lip and pause it. One of us then scrambled up the ladder and shoveled the lime to the spinning slurry inside the tank.

When the mixture reached the pH of water, the litmus strips we'd dip into the liquid turned sky-blue. At that point we could pump the stuff into a hollow scooped beside Mill Creek. The liquid did its best to seep into the soil, but a mass of colored sludge that looked like batter remained. The sludge dried, shrank, and cracked—everything below the top layer staying moist, the surface finally hardening, like a scab on the outside of a nasty wound.

When Dwayne decided to quit his job, I urged him to deploy the joke from the novel *Another Roadside Attraction*, that hallucinogenic classic set in the coastal Pacific Northwest, written by Tom Robbins when we were coming of age. One of the characters "calls in well" to work. He tells his boss he had been sick since he started the job, gotten sicker as time went by, but now that he had gotten well he'd finally decided not to show up any more.

On that triumphant night when Dwayne picked up his final check, he sped away in his blocky Datsun sedan whose side panels were corroded by the acids on the road. Raising a swirl of zinc dust, he lofted a middle-finger salute to the factory from his open window. That was the last I saw of him.

Before I got gumption enough to quit and go to college full time, Mike secured a job at a Harbor Island foundry where he worked for many years. Cleaned up his act, Mike did, to fit into that union shop and enjoy its higher wages. With a fierce red beard and hair cropped short, his belly more pronounced, he had his urine and blood tested weekly to monitor his levels of mercury and lead. Heroin had been his nemesis but he kicked it, kicked the monkey off his back.

My nemesis at Western Processing turned out to be the agricultural fertilizer zinc sulfate. Its manufacture called for pumping water and sulfuric acid into an antique cement mixer, then shoveling zinc chunks to be dissolved in the slurry when stirred by the mixer's fins. The zinc clanked and battered as it hit the baffles of the machine. The finished liquid product would get pumped into a fifty-thousand-gallon tank until trucks came to haul it away.

After some of the zinc precipitated out and settled to the tank floor, we grunts had to climb inside the container and shovel the stuff into buckets, doing our best not to breathe the fumes in the tank. If superstitious people in the Middle Ages believed they could escape the plague by snuffing a handful of petals, a "pocket full of posies," we relied on smoking cigarettes inside the narrow space of that industrial tank to rarefy the air.

Decades later, we are still learning the legacy of toxic wastes spread on farm fields under the guise of liquid fertilizer. Patty Martin, former mayor of Quincy, Washington, heard farmers "wondering aloud why their wheat yields were lousy, their corn crops thin, their cows sickly." Her investigation met conspicuous walls of opposition from industry officials. She discovered, at last, a nationwide practice of recycling hazardous wastes and selling them as fertilizers without the knowledge of the farmers who buy them.

Children in the town, their hair tested for toxins, harbored hazardously high levels of aluminum, antimony, arsenic, cadmium, and lead. Later Martin lost her job as mayor, but she won a legislative victory. Gary Locke, America's first Asian American governor, signed a Washington State bill that promised to trace those metals from factories to fertilizers so they stay out of food.

That summer night beneath the glare of the mercury-vapor yard lights, working alone at making zinc sulfate, I was too hot to be wearing the usual rain gear. Fall term was starting soon. I was sick of the job and ready to quit.

When I switched on a pump to start the acid flowing, a fitting broke, and in an instant I was drenched from crotch to knees. Switching off the wildly spraying machine, I sprinted for the bathroom. By the time I got there my pants were in rags, the plastic lighter in my pocket had melted, and the skin on my inner thighs was fried. There were no showers to irrigate my burns. I flushed my legs with water scooped from a toilet bowl by hand. Then I loaded up to drive myself to an emergency room in my antique panel truck.

Today, wearing shorts, looking at my legs in the sun, I see those faint scars. The lay of the land impresses itself on the body and the mind, and it's fitting for me to carry away marks from that job that helped to shape my early adult days. My father in his Seattle flooring business had been my mentor, and the teenage construction jobs he lined up for me served as kindergarten. The military industrial waste that Western Processing handled was my college, and old Garmt Nieuwenhuis — dodging his civic obligations long enough to have become a kind of white-collar outlaw — became my alma mater.

Edward Abbey compared society to a stew. Both have to be stirred up every so often or scum will rise to the top. The trouble is, we can't always tell the scum from the stew, the saviors from the slaves. Appearances deceive. If my government appropriates millions to clean up mistakes, who is to say what's the best way, how much cash is enough, and who should be in charge? The skeptic in me suspects that when public funds are appropriated, someone already floating near the top of that particular pot is apt to rise the higher.

Ten years after I worked at Western Processing, the EPA would shut it down. Legislation passed in the Carter era made so-called

Superfund money available, money that people had to spend to justify. Government was not in the business of cleaning up waste, it grew clear; EPA only allocated funds for cleanup. Good incomes were waiting to be made through government generosity in remediating toxic waste sites.

At the 1990 trial between Boeing and its insurers, trial participants said Boeing had been warned some sixteen times over thirty years that its waste dumping could cause contamination and was probably illegal. Boeing replied that Western Processing represented state-of-the-art hazardous waste disposal.

Newspapers ran stories of showdowns between the EPA and Luurt Nieuwenhuis, the elderly founder's successor and son. Luurt ran officials off his land. Government agencies seemed unwilling to enforce the law in earnest, loath to match their firm words with resolute acts. Greenpeace activists who entered the site to gather samples got in a shoving match with laborers inside.

The chairman of a congressional committee reviled Boeing and other defense contractors for "charging taxpayers to clean up dump sites that they helped pollute." Pentagon suppliers long have let the public foot the bill to remediate messes they created, charged John Conyers, the Michigan Democrat who surprised the Senate with his testimony. Government Accounting Office records show that corporations build goodwill by taking charge of cleaning up such sites, but end up submitting heavy reimbursement claims to taxpayers.

This flawed system gives little incentive for contractors to develop environmentally safer processes in the first place. If they can profit and claim tax write-offs from polluting, companies do not need to change their ways.

At the Site Remediation Office for Western Processing, Herb Gaskell told me only a partial truth when he claimed that his employer, the Boeing Company, was footing seventy-eight percent of the clean-up costs. If history repeats, Boeing's expenses will end as write-offs, the cost of doing business. Then, too, there are the inestimable costs to the local ecology to factor in. Herb Gaskell, weary and glum at seeing his career come to such a humiliating end, might be willing to acknowledge the baseness of his cause, were he alive. Far from doing the right thing for sound reasons, defense contractors across decades have learned that doing the wrong thing by way of the environment and the American public almost always garners material rewards.

Knowing that my interest was keen, Herb Gaskell invited me to write a history of Western Processing that Boeing could lay claim to, a narrative the company could possess. The pay would be good, he intimated. The views at the site were much improved, the mounds of zinc dust vanished, the acid ponds drained away. Ducks swam and dabbled beside shoots of grass that shot from topsoil spread over the damaged land. Fresh out of college, and with no job prospects, I was tempted by Herb's offer. After I turned it over, though, I told Herb no. I would not help remediate Boeing's ill fame.

I would wait, I decided. I would tell all the truth but tell it slant, as Emily Dickinson phrased it. Instead of composing an industry-sponsored chronicle, I would wait to write the story on my own terms and time. Better to hold off, compose a history for fathers and sons, for my own fond father newly fallen from cancer, for my own children and their scarred dad. My history would report on an industrial abundance, a landscape whose face held human shapes, and a city that rose from illness to draw deep breaths again.

# Three Coyotes

S
ometime prior to 1830, Pacific Northwest tribes created the Chinook jargon, a trading language to help them skirt the intricacies of their dialects and barter for goods with one another. White fur traders adopted the jargon as well, inspiring even greater use of that bastard vernacular. A trading frenzy ensued. Indians began to forget their Coast Salish dialects. In turn they began to lose touch with the folkways and cultures embedded in those words. The Chinook jargon—as traveler Theodore Winthrop typified it, with what passed in his era for wit—"was an attempt on a small scale to nullify Babel by combining a confusion of tongues into a confounding of tongues."

Winthrop practiced the jargon when he traveled Washington Territory in 1853. He trained his eyes on the literary trade, and especially on east coast readers whose interest in natives, barbarians, savages, siwashes, or aborigines by any other name might impart an authentic scent to help him sell his books.

His forebears had received the genes of stern New England puritans, including the first governor of the Massachusetts Bay Colony, John Winthrop. Theodore wielded his illustrious Winthrop name like a weapon, inscribing wide arcs with it everywhere he went. The North Cascades town of Winthrop adopted his name in the 1890s, as did the Winthrop Glacier on Mount Rainier that he valorized in the best of his books.

The S'Klallam and Yakama people whom he hired, bullied, insulted, and harangued had never heard of him, though. His pretense of aristocracy was lost on them. His attempts to cultivate them failed. He was adrift on the frontier, "seeking my fortune," as he said by letter to his widowed mother on Staten Island. He rejoined her late in 1853, after a year spent on the frontier as a speculator, a privileged tourist, and an incidental agent of expansion. In a rented New York City studio in 1854, he settled in to writing his five books.

One hundred and fifty years after Winthrop's visit, on a bluff above the Columbia River, a coyote was nosing through a field of bunch-grass. It paused, listened, sniffed, and drifted to another tuft. It looked less like the trickster of Native myth than a domestic dog. Willows and locust trees lined a dry creek bed there. The roots of those trees, shallow and dry as summer dust, had burnt to the hollow of an Au-gust drought that was scorching the land there by Mount Adams in Washington State, across from the Oregon town The Dalles.

Fort Dalles, founded in 1850 as the only Army post between Wyo-ming and Puget Sound, aimed to quell the "Indian disturbances" dis-tressing settlers in the eastern reaches of that newly minted Washing-ton Territory. For centuries the natives had known the site only as Win-Quatt, a name settlers found less fetching than *dalles*, which is French for paving stone. Today the Oregon town houses the National Socialist Vanguard, a small neo-Nazi group that plants racist seeds in an effort to harvest true believers in its cause.

Our hot car ground to a halt on the shoulder of the gravel road above the coyote. The animal kept on hunting as if oblivious to us — to Karen, our two young boys, and me behind the tinted glass. The coyote reared and plunged, forelegs stiff, back arched — its nose an arrow aimed to skewer some small fur in the grass. Its ears swiv-eled, feet minced. This hunting looked like fun from our vantage point a hundred yards away. Transforming into a graceful curve, the coyote hopped a ditch, and at last our two-year-old son in his car seat caught sight of it. Chase shrieked, bounced, and imitated the pounce in his car seat, pointing his arms and hands as if they were forelegs and paws.

We were traveling blue highways in our car to trace the same path that Winthrop traveled on horseback. Karen had agreed to this hot and dusty trip in large part to humor me in my obsession. She was caring for our children as I took photos and wrote in my journal on a campstool every day at dusk. Besides rearing the children with me, she has her own career to nurture, as a public defender for the state and federal government. She does God's work, as one of our wise friends put it. She is the partner I have always hoped for, generous and gentle and nonjudgmental. Together we were heading back to 1853 when Washington became a territory, when it splintered from Oregon Territory to accommodate the growing population in its regions surrounding Puget Sound.

On our trip that August we met with three coyotes. The first one hunted among tufts of bunchgrass, its snout to the ground. The second one turned its top lip inside out, warning us away. The third one slunk in disgrace among fishery wharves in a shallow bay, stopping to fidget and nip its hairless back.

Theodore Winthrop, my spirit guide, was not Washington Territory's first tourist, but he wrote most memorably about its mountains and waters. He admired nature but scorned the indigenous people he met in the territory. His travel book *The Canoe and the Saddle,* a model of early Pacific Northwest nature writing, blisters his Indian guides by calling into question their characters, canoes, hygiene, language, food, and dress. Those two sides of his personality, the nature-lover and the bigot, are tough for modern readers to square.

A tenderfoot, he had graduated from Yale and enjoyed a grand tour of Europe to put a finishing touch on his gentleman's profile. Later he served as a clerk in Panama's jungles until the climate proved too taxing for his health. By the time he got to the Pacific Northwest, he had adopted another persona. He was a "merciful rider of nine stone weight," he wrote, one who wore a big red beard that helped him swell beyond his meager 126 pounds. He rode a fiery horse and shoved around his weight with the assistance of a Colt sidearm.

Attentive to rivers and peaks, horses and alpine storms, he was cruel to the native people. He kicked and insulted them. He hired paddlers from the S'Klallam tribe to traverse the length of Puget Sound. At Fort Nisqually, near today's Tacoma, he recruited a Klickitat or Yakama scout, and he bought three horses to hoof it overland. He paid, in Hudson's Bay Company shirts and blankets, to get to the Oregon Trail he would take home.

I had grown fixated, not on him but on the Indians whom he tangled with along the way. I was bent on reversing his route in the book, traveling from the Oregon Trail by way of the Naches Trail northward toward Puget Sound. For two hot days we camped in Washington State by the west fork of the White River. Where we splashed and played, the Connecticut Yankee had fed, slept, and booted his nineteen-year-old guide to rouse him from his bed. Such a *coup de pied*, clueless and rude, proved a poisonous insult to the Indians of that time. It demonstrated a measure of Winthrop's self-appointed superiority and disdain.

During our second day in camp, in the late afternoon, we heard a distant coyote begin to howl. Strange, we thought. In the skin of our thin experience, coyotes howled only at night. Its yips and yodels grew closer. Dusk began to fall, and still that agitated coyote's cries came on. We built a roaring campfire.

The Washington Territory, where Winthrop spent the most time during his six-month tour of the Pacific Northwest, was a place of ecological and racial turmoil. Indians were dying from diseases, bullets, and drink, their economies altered forever by white contact, their lands and lore usurped and ridiculed. Lumber vessels loaded with fir trees, to be sunk as piles to make San Francisco docks, were already thronging the waters of Puget Sound. Gold miners were raking hillsides and creek beds. Would-be barons were carving out big farms.

Winthrop alludes to few of these tensions, even though he traveled some three hundred miles among the S'Klallams and Klickitats, whose tribal names he planned to use to title his book until a Minié ball, fired by a Confederate soldier in the Civil War, eclipsed his plans for future fame and ended his short life. His editors in Boston titled his book for him, calling it *The Canoe and the Saddle*.

Wild animals will bare their teeth or yelp to frighten trespassers away. The intended effect of such animal behavior is to make the interloper edgy. We had seen coyotes pace or chase dogs and people, curling the upper lip so far back the jaw appeared unhinged. In a wildlife refuge, a coyote had circled and spooked us, managing to remain invisible in bushes the whole while it did, pacing us for a quarter mile to let us know we needed to leave.

In the same way, whitetail deer had worked to bluff me from a plum grove where I spent a fitful night on the Palouse in Idaho. Their huffs, snorts, and ghostly wheezes woke me with a start. I stiffened in my hammock, my eyes grew wide, but I saw nothing. They huffed, stamped, circled my bed. Chilled, I lay quiet as death. What manner of unseen beings were wanting me to leave?

Camping on Winthrop's route, we knew it was a coyote prowling just outside our campfire's light. We had heard it howling a long way away. In thick brush it took its stand, squealing and growling, clacking its teeth to underscore the dire intent. Maybe it was rabid, we worried, apt to rush us. I caught one thin glimpse of a top lip curled so far it looked like a fruit rind coming off. There would be little sleeping that night if its harangue kept up.

Winthrop had dangled a pistol by a lanyard from his saddle horn. One day, hunting for grouse along the Naches River, he blasted a black bear with birdshot, a foolish move. The wounded animal took a swing at him then fled. That pistol, a six-shooter, a cap-and-ball Colt Navy revolver, came in handy aboard the canoe he hired to pilot him eighty-five miles down Puget Sound.

In the boat he ordered his paddlers to work, he seized their rum to keep them in line, and he flourished the Colt to thwart their uprising. "Look down this muzzle," he claimed to have said to them with cool bravado, "as I whisk it about and bring it to bear on each of you in turn." Like Malvolio in Shakespeare's *Twelfth Night*, this descendent of New England Puritans might have thought that because he was so virtuous there ought to be no more cakes and ale.

Karen and I, in the golden era before small children, used to camp and hike a lot. In windy Montana and Wyoming breaks, grizzly country, she had been too tense to sleep. And so I packed along a big handgun, a stainless steel Smith and Wesson .357, a six-shooter stenciled with the name of the Coeur d'Alene policeman in Idaho who had liquidated the revolver in an upgrade.

In eastern Montana, during tornado season, a thunderstorm passed by us very close one night. The lightning's flash and thunder's crack were simultaneous events. The ribs of our tent poles shone through the nylon sheath like a thin red skin. That cannon of a pistol in the backpack, that tool I had toted along for safety's sake, afforded us no respite from the storm.

Beside the White River I drew that big sidearm—it pains me to admit—just outside of Mount Rainier National Park. I fired a shot above the unseen coyote's head, hoping to frighten it away. The slug rattled the brush, but the teeth kept gnashing. I did not fire a second time. The animal won. It evicted us. We flung tent and bags and children in the car and drove back out the rocky road after dark. We never learned the cause of its explosive mood. We only knew it did not wish for us to stay. That place, its home, was not ours.

Biologists told us later that we had probably set our camp up on its den. The pups had spent the first night alone, or visited by a crafty parent while we slept, but a second night would have been too much. We had to be scared away. We agreed to leave, relinquish that place to its fierce tenants.

Lots of bloodshed stained the early pioneer days. Members of the Cayuse tribe murdered missionaries Marcus and Narcissa Whitman and their kids in Walla Walla in 1847. In 1858, soldiers killed Yakama chief Owhi near Fort Dalles, shot him in the back. He was never implicated in the Whitman murders, but he had led a running rebellion against the white occupiers of his lands. Owhi's son, Qualchan, was tricked into a military camp and lynched after clashes with white militia. Winthrop hired another one of Chief Owhi's sons to guide him across the Naches Pass en route to Fort Dalles in 1853.

That son—variously named Loolowcan, L'Quoit or Lo-kout—outlived Winthrop by fifty years. He became a sniper in the Yakama Wars that began in 1855. Like the robed defenders of mountain villages of Afghanistan today, Lo-kout shot invaders at a distance with a rifle imported from afar. Wounded in a battlefield, hit in the chest, Lo-kout passed out, lay on the dirt. A soldier struck him in the forehead with a gun butt, crushing his skull and leaving him for dead. He told his story in 1906, fiery even in his eighties. Bearing a concave goose egg on his brow, he said he wished he had murdered Winthrop.

Photos of that Indian guide, that aged warrior, have agitated my rest. In one he poses with eyes closed, kneeling as if in prayer; gray braids fall to his waist. A round hat, with a rattlesnake band, shades one thigh. He looks weary. Another shot—this one taken by Edward Sheriff Curtis, the famous photographer who posed the Indians for his gorgeous portraits—shows Lo-kout in noble profile, his chin elevated as if to regard some far-off scene, hair combed down to hide the forehead gouge, his every feature golden as a god's, washed by the trademark Curtis orotone. In yet another photo, this one from archives of the Spokane Tribe, Lo-kout is in ceremonial regalia, posing with his grandson, both of them on horseback. Lo-kout's face is turned away.

By August 21, 1853, Theodore Winthrop was ending his Pacific Northwest tour. He had gone through Portland, Astoria, The Dalles,

Cowlitz, Vancouver, Olympia, Bellingham, and Victoria. If he had not managed to gain the fortune he was seeking, he had at least hobnobbed with Hudson's Bay Company merchants and Army officers along the way. Washington Irving had penned a flattering biography of Captain Bonneville that sold well; maybe, Winthrop thought, he could also memorialize some mover and shaker of the American empire.

At Port Townsend, in northern Puget Sound, he demanded a canoe and paddlers to take him to Fort Nisqually, in the southern reaches of Puget Sound. He was short on time, agitated, and impatient to leave. Residents of the small town directed him to two brothers, both of them leaders of the S'Klallam tribe, named King George and the Duke of York.

King George had a boat, but he was drunk and snoring, too far gone to be awakened. Winthrop was ready to seize the boat and draft some paddlers, by barrel-force if need be. He was going to have his way. "I became wroth," he wrote, "and, advancing where the king of all this region lay, limp, stertorous, and futile, I kicked him liberally." He crowed about his boldness in his memoir. "Yes! I have kicked a king." Winthrop had some imperial fun. After the boot-blow, King George rose long enough to wave a knife in Winthrop's face, then fell back to sleep, oblivious of the breach of common courtesy.

White settlers and tourists liked to bestow the names of British royalty on Indians as a form of mockery. The Natives might have been willing to tolerate the mockery, as it freed them of the need to relinquish their given names. Some of them regarded the surrender of their names as a hazard, an act of potential defeat. One who knows your name may inflict much greater injury, as today's celebrities hounded by the paparazzi will confirm.

King George's brother, dubbed the Duke of York, was in fact named Chetzemoka, a wise and able leader who guided a large tribe on Puget Sound. History shows his tribe to have been mostly friendly to white settlers. Winthrop, though, with overwhelming cultural superiority, characterized Chetzemoka as "a drunken rascal, a shameless liar, a thief."

The year after Winthrop visited, Chetzemoka became hereditary chief of the tribe and held that title until 1876. His wives, See-hem-itza and Chill'lil, were nicknamed Queen Victoria and Jenny Lind. Two years after he met Winthrop, Chetzemoka signed the Treaty of Point

No Point, which became a compelling legal basis in the late twentieth century for removing the Elwha and Glines Canyon dams to restore damaged salmon runs.

One photo from the era shows Chetzemoka dressed in suit jacket and hat, his chest outthrust, his eyes appraising the photographer with a mix of distrust and pride. "Civilization came, with stepmother kindness," Winthrop wrote of Chetzemoka, "baptized him with rum, clothed him in discarded slops, and dubbed him the Duke of York." Later invaders, some of them no doubt ancestors on my father's side from Scandinavia, applied his name to a Puget Sound ferryboat and a Port Townsend park.

Winthrop, almost frantic, had to leave that day. The word spread that he would give trinkets and Hudson's Bay blankets—one for each Indian who paddled, another for the owner of the boat. The canoe he finally hired, "the leaky better of two vessels," was a handsome bit of engineering—a forty-foot dugout carved of a whole cedar trunk, its outer edge stained red and embedded with shells. Before first contact with Europeans had introduced metal tools to the tribes, clamshell scrapers shaped and hollowed each canoe. Port Gamble S'Klallam people now are reviving the crafting of those boats.

Winthrop found it tough to show gratitude or appreciation for the loan of the craft, though. A row of shells "inserted in the gunwale served as talismans against Bugaboo," he wrote. Like a boogeyman, the bugaboo was a baseless fear, a bugbear. The Natives in their pagan faith were akin to silly kids. This assessment of their religion from a man who was suffering seven generations later from the Puritan pathologies of his ancestor John Winthrop, the first governor of the Massachusetts Bay Colony, a lawyer who persecuted Quaker evangelists and supported the extirpation of the entire Pequot tribe.

Theodore Winthrop's paddlers, from feeding on wild salmon, "were oozier with its juices than I could wish of people I must touch and smell for a voyage of two days." Ever fastidious, Winthrop reminded his readers he was slumming among "unsavory, hickory-shirted, mat-haired, truculent siwashes."

Once his paddlers learned who was boss, Winthrop was free to enjoy the scenery, and so Mount Rainier comes in for pages of description and praise. He also makes sage observations as a naturalist. Mount Saint Helens, which would erupt with force 127 years later, "showers her realms with a boon of light ashes, to notify them that her peace is repose, not stupor; and sometimes she lifts a tremulous flame by night from her summit." Tourists would profit from his wisdom, he believed, once immigration got rolling and the "attempt is made to manage Pagan savages."

His guide, the "low-browed Loolowcan"—more specifically a "half-insolent, half-indifferent, jargoning savage"—had a "superstitious soul," much like gibbering Jim, the escaped slave whom Huckleberry Finn duped but loved.

Every observation Winthrop made of indigenous religion was flippant or dismissive. He lashed the Indians with nasty epithets. He interpreted their displays of faith as irrational fear. And yet he displayed a Christian double standard when he swooned over oblate Catholic missionaries in their mud huts near Yakima. His tone may help explain why it took the U.S. justice system until 1978 to pass the American Indian Religious Freedom Act into law.

After canoeing for two days down Puget Sound, Winthrop arrived at Fort Nisqually and paid off his S'Klallam guides. He was in a huff to head out. With the help of Owhi, that foremost chief in the Yakama tribe, Winthrop hired the chief's son, Lo-kout, to take him across the Cascades. At the fort's store he purchased pork, hard-tack, and three mustangs, then hit the Naches Trail bound for Fort Dalles, more than two hundred miles away.

The going was rough, laced with trees felled by military engineers. Like the men who had felled them, Winthrop understood that "destruction precedes reconstruction." Trees and Indians alike must be made to die into life. With a nod to the kinship between the Klickitat tribespeople and the land, he noted, "this was a transition period. In the Cascades, Klickitat institutions were toppling, Boston notions coming in," for Indians knew whites as Bostons and aimed to emulate them. Winthrop was irascible all the same. The mustangs he bought were giving him trouble, and time was eluding his need for control.

Throughout all these exploits, he insisted on an identity as a fastidious ambassador of high culture, a minister of the spiritual arts. Stowed in his saddlebags were fine shirts, breeches, and hats. He aimed to enlighten the Indians and thereby leaven the frequent episodes of *barbarism*, as he named it, among them. He bought a salmon to cook on the trail and wrote, "how much better than feeding foul Indians it was to belong to me, who would treat his proportions with respect, feel the exquisiteness of his coloring, grill him delicately, and eat him daintily!" In the purple passages of his travelogue he celebrated nature's glories, he waxed ecstatic in their fine light, until the blackness of his ailing Puritan soul intruded once again.

Like many of his forebears, Winthrop had long struggled with his faith. During his college years he underwent a religious conversion, during which he spent so many hours praying in his room that his sisters feared he was losing his mind. In later years, "nervous exhaustion, vague and untraceable illnesses, stomach pains, and recurring attacks of crushing despondency" shadowed his periods of sociability and feverish pleasure. When he confessed to his mother in a letter that his belief in Christianity was faltering, she grieved to family and friends, and the globetrotting Theodore became much gossiped about in the drawing rooms of New York, New Haven, Newport, and Boston.

Weary in the high Cascades, a foul mood seized him and he kicked Lo-kout to rouse him from bed. Threatened, insulted, bruised, and coerced, Lo-kout deserted the Yankee, leaving him to guide himself to Fort Dalles where he was to meet his traveling companions for the horseback ride on the Oregon Trail back home. And so Winthrop spent a drenched and restless night in a thunderstorm alone. On a high prairie near present-day Selah, he lit a hollow tree on fire to keep warm. It toppled while he was drowsing, almost did him in. The next day, ill from exposure, he passed out and tumbled from his horse.

Fifty-three years later Lo-kout, the guide who abandoned Winthrop on that prairie in the Yakima Valley, was found and interviewed by historian A. J. Splawn. It was 1906. Lo-kout was living with his hanged brother's widow, whom he had taken as his wife, at a spot where the Spokane River forms a confluence with the Columbia River. Asked if he was the same Loolowcan of that journey, the man quickly rose to his feet and, "with flashing eyes," he said, "Yes, I was then Loolowcan, but I changed my name during the war later." The mere mention of Winthrop's name triggered all the tension once again.

In 1858, his wife, named Whist-alks, drove a lance into the earth when it grew plain the soldiers aimed to hang her first husband, Qualchan. She wheeled her horse and dashed away. Lo-kout rode with her, lucky to escape with his life, relying on the phony testimony of a friend who claimed Lo-kout was not Qualchan's brother. Widowered in 1906, he revealed that his grief and anger smoldered still. Seven bullets had pierced him. His forehead crushed, his brother hanged, his people scattered, his father shot, he had found refuge with a neutral tribe, the Spokanes, by virtue of his wife's birthright.

Lo-kout said of Winthrop, in language Winthrop's book confirms, "I did not like the man's looks and said so, but was ordered to get ready and start. He soon began to get cross and the farther we went the worse he got, and the night we stayed at the white men's camp who were working on the road in the mountains, he kicked me with his boot as if I was a dog. When we arrived at Wenas Creek, where some of our people were camped, I refused to go farther; he drew his revolver and told me I had to go with him to The Dalles. I would have killed him only for my cousin and aunt. I have often thought of that man and regretted I did not kill him. He was *me-satch-ee* (mean)."

These details line up with Winthrop's behavior as related in *The Canoe and the Saddle*—acting moody, insulting his scout, delivering a kick while he slept, flashing his gun. Through his writing he could turn his focus away from dominating his Indian guides and instead to involving himself in describing nature as a transcendent space that his command of language gave him power to rule.

Winding along the shores of Puget Sound, camping and swimming with our two little children in the hottest month of the year, Karen and I met with a final coyote. It seemed to be our destiny, as we traced Winthrop's route, to meet one every hundred miles along our way. This last animal had become a resident of the bay, a gloomy ghost, a wretched genius locus engrossed by scrounging the Bellingham waterfront. I gave a shudder for my adult son Braden, gone missing two years earlier while kayaking in that same bay.

Winthrop had toured coal mines there. He had contemplated buying into those mines to earn the fortune he was convinced Earth owed him. He took a canoe trip toward Victoria, British Columbia, and watched William Fraser Tolmie vaccinate Nooksack Indians against smallpox. Tolmie's altruism did not help to soften Winthrop's ethnocentrism, though; his bad attitude toward the Indians remains the starkest part of his otherwise appealing book.

As a literate commentator on the nineteenth-century American West, Winthrop told the truth in partial and partisan terms. Still, "the story of a civilized man's solitary onslaught at barbarism cannot lose its interest," he wrote, in language that many amateur historians would still applaud today. Chauvinist pride in the Pacific Northwest has vaulted him and his writing to the top ranks of regional travel writers. His rhapsodic take on nature, his defensive splendor, screened off the territory's violent cultural transformations that he helped create.

When we arrived at Squalicum Harbor that August day, it was hot and everything stunk. Seafood canneries were weeping fishy liquors. Our eyes watered from the stench. On the shore a shabby coyote was skulking after cannery scraps, moving in and out of shadows. Where its species used to den, the new Bellis Fair Mall shone its neon signs at night from miles away.

Summer's heat had blasted the coyote's fur—heat and mange and a rampage of fleas. Its back was pink, scabbed, almost hairless. Crab claws dropped from the freight cars moldered. Fish offal hosed off the long piers fumed. If the coyote accepted such refuse, a bond would be born, what was wild would certainly turn tame, or so the smoking laborers at the cannery maintained.

# The Way to Open

Off Lopez Island, two otters rolled and dove for abalone. They pried those muscles of suction from boulders beneath the waves of Puget Sound. Earthbound on shore, I lifted up an empty abalone shell. Pearly mother light inside its hollow cast back my shadow, and the sky behind me gathered hue. All whiskers and dog-jowls, the otters watched me over their shoulders and swam farther out to sea. I yearned to slide beside them and recover something I'd mislaid. There is this shell inside us no one knows the way to open.

Hundreds of miles inland and several years later, the sun was rising on the Salmon River of Idaho. My fellow travelers and I were feeling dim as we broke camp and loaded the boats. Some of us had drunk too much beer the evening before, and thunderstorms had jolted us awake all night. To worsen our moods, lots of spiders were afoot on the sandbar, creeping us out, making me eager to shove off from terra firma and head downstream. I bent to pick up a wrapper we'd dropped; one of the spiders dashed before me, followed by a long-legged wasp. I hunkered down to watch the show unfold.

The spider flipped on its back to fend off its attacker, all eight legs flailing in the air, then righted itself and whirled away, a spinning quarter on a dance floor. The nimble wasp grappled closer, pressing its advantage from the air. I had seen such wasps before—flicking wings, hopping on long legs, twitching and fidgeting—but I'd never seen one so focused.

It pinned the spider, bent at the waist, and probed with a stinger, striving to drive home the stunning stroke. Once again the spider rose to wheel across the sand. A few more tumbles and sprints and the wasp got its way. Aiming its weight, restraining its prey, it injected a protein cocktail.

It was a female spider wasp, one of forty-two hundred species around the planet that prey on arachnids, one of three hundred in North America alone. Only the female of the species pursues the spiders. Only the female stings and stuns the prey, with the help of a modified ovipositor, the tubular organ also used for laying eggs.

Afterward she drags the immobile spider to a burrow or dried mud chamber. She crams it in by body-force, lays an egg, and sometimes clips the legs. Severing the spider's legs prevents it from escaping the cell, which serves as nursery for the wasp offspring. Once the orange egg hatches, the spider becomes a living host, a succulent lunch. The blind white larva shoulders its way out of the egg sac, spins a silky thin cocoon, and pupates beside the spider's crumbling husk. When at last the wings start coming on, the new wasp chips away the sand or mud and emerges to the world.

I did not have time to see the mother wasp stuff the spider in her nest that day. My raft-mates were waiting for me, and I had a paddle to ply.

Our trip down the Salmon River in central Idaho had a public function: to restore the river ecosystem. Eight of us volunteers, from towns around the northern Rockies, were teaming with three forest rangers to traverse that largest designated wild area in the lower forty-eight states, the Frank Church River of No Return Wilderness, on a trip of eighty miles. Three specialists from the Slate Creek Ranger Station outside Riggins, Idaho—two patrol rangers and a range conservationist—were guiding us for the week.

On the trip we aimed to slow the spread of spotted knapweed, a stalk of exotic vegetation, an invasive thistle from Eastern Europe that has prospered across many millions of acres in the American West following its launch in a load of tainted alfalfa. Knapweed, alleopathic, generates chemicals suited only to its kind. The prickly plant poisons the surrounding soil. It spreads toxins that cause other vegetation slowly to die off. Every knapweed stalk also broadcasts up to a thousand seeds that remain fertile for five years. They do their best to spread their range by hitching rides downstream. After uprooting the stalks by hand, fingers that touched our mouths or eyes made us pucker and feel stung.

While serving my part in the river restoration, I had another project all my own—to get personal with the medium of water, following my son's death by drowning. Braden had vanished three years before while kayaking with a friend in Puget Sound. Their bodies were never found.

I still struggled with crippling doubts about how they went down. A kind of hydro-nausea welled up when I neared big water. At times I even imagined I heard his voice cry out, as if from some great distance. And in the movements of my fellow paddlers, one of them about his age, I could see a gesture of his I pined for—an edgy and awkward flick of the wrist.

A dose of nature, a sample of its hazards, might alleviate my grief, I reasoned, in much the same way that the petty jab of an injection is meant to stave off greater pain. A paddling trip into this wilderness might restore my tortured core, I told myself. First a little, then some more, I would savor nature's dangerous hoard. I would invite the water to open up my pores.

For eighty-five hundred years the Nez Perce and Sheepeater Shoshones lived in the Salmon River Canyon, feeding on salmon and bighorn sheep. When Lewis and Clark came through, those natives advised Captain William Clark that the canyon was impassable to the Pacific. But Clark needed to see for himself.

Sizing up the riverbank on August 23, 1805, Clark found rocks "so sharp large and unsettled and the hill sides Steep that the horses could with the greatest risque and difficulty get on." The canyon was treacherous because "the water is Confined between huge Rocks & the current beeting from one against another for Some distance below." The storied Northwest Passage it was not. Clark chose another route to the Pacific for his Corps of Discovery.

The Indians dressed furs skillfully, a talent that helped them survive harsh winters. Rounded up by the U.S. military in 1879, defeated without much fight, they trekked under threat of force to what is now Fort Hall Reservation, two hundred eighty miles away in southern Idaho. On granite walls beside the river they left pictographs in red ochre—hydrated iron oxide. A horse here, a shield design there, still visited and refreshed by descendents from Fort Hall. My paddling partners posed for photos before the old rock art.

In keeping with its protected status since 1980, the River of No Return Wilderness outlaws access by motorized vehicles, even though its founder, Senator Frank Church, had to grandfather a few jet-boat lines into the deal. Church preserved it as wilderness despite a conservative tide of opinion that soon would flood the state of Idaho. Upon his death in 1984, the two-and-a-half million acres were named in his honor. The Wilderness, Church knew, protects material culture like pictographs, cabins, and wooden scows with sweep blades. It confers wisdom about how to survive big water, bad weather, predators, and falling rocks.

Our first night out, after a long trip on rutted roads, we arrived after 1:00 AM. Thunder was rumbling, lightning flashing, drenching rain a threat. The storm held off, but wind gusts flapped our tarps and slashed the fabric of our sleep. Our rangers were stirring early, though — stowing gear, brewing coffee, urging us to rise. We twitched in our bags, rubbed dust in our hair.

Linda offered us mugs of coffee. I had heard about her before we ever met. Like me she is a vegetarian, I had heard, and I hoped we would hit it off. A head-wrap of Buddhist prayer flags held her hair, graying above and brown below, girlishly pigtailed. She hails from West Virginia, an origin betrayed in the long vowels she mouths. Her lingering southern lilt proved lovely to my ears, all the more so when I saw her sling ten-foot saplings aside to tidy a site for the cook stoves. She had been "a gnarly feminist" in the 1970s, she admitted when we had a chance to talk. When her marriage ended, she began guiding tourists and dudes down the Snake and Salmon rivers.

"Why are you a vegetarian?" I asked. I had heard she'd be counting on us other meatless eaters, and I know that motives for eschewing meat are many. Linda pushed some hair away from her face, pondered my question, narrowed her eyes, and glanced toward Howard — the range conservationist, the liaison between the public-land ranchers and the feds. Howard had done the shopping for the trip, filling ice chests with bacon and sausage, steaks and chops. A squall blew off the water. Big pines trees bent above our heads.

"I'm an animal person," she whispered, language code for animal-rights sympathizer or activist. I nodded my head to let her know I understood exactly what she meant. Later Linda refused to eat the salmon Howard grilled — the only one among us to reject it. She had socked in boxes of soy patties. In her presence I felt hypocritical, compromised, a lacto-ovo-pesco vegetarian.

Linda carried over a gruff manner from the 1970s. Piloting her heavy oar rig, she braced feet on the aluminum frame to navigate the biggest rapids and turns. She faced downstream. Unless the wind stiffened or current slackened, she shoved the oars to direct the boat. She relied more on elegance than on strength to get by. I admired her from a distance and kept my big mouth shut.

We volunteers paddled on a raft that had no frame. It could wrap itself around a rock if the current pinned it wrong. We paddlers needed to throw our shoulders into the effort and stroke our hardest when about to mount a standing wave; we had to gain force and momentum before plunging into the watery trough that follows. To ply a paddle with too little vigor would be to risk being dubbed a teabagger—one who lazes, drowses, dabbles at his task—an aristocrat dipping a teabag in a cup and pointing a pinkie finger for balance.

On the water that first day, we headed into the Bargamin-Bailey Circus—as Linda fondly called it—the rapids that link Bargamin Creek and Bailey Bar. Flush with runoff, the waves reared higher than their class IV ranking indicated on the maps. Like a rush from robust drugs, stretches of extreme whitewater pump endorphin levels up. We were primed, ready to ride.

"Linda, should we get out and scout this rapid first?" Ron shouted.

"No, just read it and run it."

To read it, she stood high in her raft above the rapids and scanned the waves with a practiced eye. Bringing up the rear in the paddleboat, piercing the foam and entering the roar, we followed Linda's line, mimicked her smooth moves.

While Linda and her passenger rode safe and dry, we got slammed in the face by doors of water again and again. Smaller and less waterworthy, our craft lunged like a bronco with a flank strap chafing. On one very bad rapid when a great wave bucked us, I cracked heads with Sierra Club staffer Jessica Reuerwhein. We saw stars, whispered sorry. Teeth chattered and bruises grew in the hours following our cohort's plunge through that set of rapids. We shared clothing drawn from dry bags, kept tabs on one another's vital signs.

That first night out we camped on Lantz Bar, named after Frank Lantz, who ran the river before World War I and never managed to shake his elation. Following the armistice, he returned with a spruce-new boat and got knocked unconscious in Gunbarrel Rapid. His lucky body eddied out face up. When Lantz came to, his dog and his boat both gone, he scrambled seventy-five miles to the town of Salmon, collected on an old debt owed him, hiked back, found his dog and the wreckage of the sweep scow. There he built a cabin from the scow planks and sawn logs and lived from 1925 to 1971.

In Lantz's neglected orchards, we rooted up new knapweed and helped ourselves to pie cherries. Old ghosts that roamed the broken outbuildings had toppled parts of the split-rail fence. Atop a stubby pine, an oriole whistled a song of contentment to the tune of exotic fruit. Things got livelier before dusk, when coyotes began to call nearby and a rattlesnake crossed a trail adjacent to our camp. I unfolded my large tarp and spread it as ground cover beneath the miscellaneous planets, suns, and galaxies that seemed to hum a subtle music.

Whatever does not sing like an oriole will be apt to prick, bite, or sting in the Salmon River Canyon. Sunburn, loose rocks, heat stroke, scorpions, thorn trees, spiders, rapids, and bizarre bugs threaten. If the water does not black you out, a clunk on the head from a loose rock might. Dodging poison ivy on a steep riverbank while pulling weeds, I dislodged a log that rolled toward the water. It bruised and almost broke my leg. Everywhere we went we met with waters that shifted their character by the moment. As if undergoing liquid mood swings, the rapids turned fearsome when unseen hydraulics changed.

I reached, dug, yanked, and piled weeds. As I did so, I observed myself in the act of carrying on my father's work. Moving past his Seattle garden to this wild in central Idaho, I was helping still to rebuild an indigenous plant community, pushing along the conservation work he had started long before.

At several of the campsites we discovered river booty, or so our pirate-guides named it. Valuables—whether swirling in currents, lodged in rocks or river sand, lost or chucked or plain forgotten—came under the law of finders-keepers. Our rangers gleaned books, watches, shirts, caps, and good food from abandoned camps. One drenched rag tore me: it reminded me of Braden's watch cap that had washed up on a beach in Puget Sound. The water gods, I felt, always aim to capsize boats, eject paddlers, lay claim to tributary gifts.

Our camp on the second night held a cockeyed wooden marker for Jack Ranger, who perished in the river in 1925. He foolishly tried to challenge the current by swimming to fetch a bighorn sheep he'd shot. The guides called the site Teepee Creek. I could imagine how he gave up the ghost. One time in the Columbia River, I thought to take a swim in a pair of pants and learned to appreciate how quickly a clad swimmer can go down. Historians of the Salmon catalog dozens of victims, travelers who took their chances and lost.

The stories and the waves kept my loss fresh. Braden must have tried to swim with his clothes on when the saltwater waves overset him in Bellingham Bay. He was wearing basketball shoes, white cotton pants, and a nylon parka.

But I was finished talking about the event, I swore. It was over and I was done. I did not want to behave like the ancient mariner—collaring others, piercing them with my eyes, waylaying strangers to hear my gruesome tale.

Forest Service policies require that rangers dismantle fire rings, toss rocks into deep water, scatter charred wood remains, and create an illusion of virgin shores. As deputy rangers, that was how we worked to naturalize a site. The Wilderness Act of 1964 makes humans "only visitors" in designated wild lands. Every trace of humans needs to be captured, hidden, held, or "broadcast," this last denoting a dispersal of toothpaste and detergents above high water lines.

We humans love the wilderness—love it to death with lug-soled boots. We scatter technology, trash, and our own plump population numbers. Every group of campers in the River of No Return Wilderness need haul along a sealed latrine, its contents emptied in a scat machine in town, a stipulation of formal Wilderness designations everywhere. River rats call such latrines groovers, from grooves pressed on ass flesh by Army ammunition cans that served during bygone days. Urine, typically aseptic, is sent swirling down the current.

Globalization means native species everywhere are facing greater risks. We mobile humans accidentally spread zebra mussels, kudzu vines, and spotted knapweed that overtake pristine habitats. Like the nonnative brown rats that throng North America's coasts, many alien invaders got their start by stowing away on waterborne cargo.

The Idaho high country is akin to Hawai'i — an isolated niche, a bio-geographic island landlocked by big mountains and swift water. Its vegetative interlopers are growing more adapted every year.

Ranger Don Jeffery has graying curly blonde hair, lapping over the ears and receding in front, set off by a cowboy mustache below. When he grins his teeth buck, his cheeks bunch like plums, his blue eyes crinkle and squint. Don and I were eddying out of the current to tidy up a beach. One of my jobs was to help land the oar rig — crouch low in the bow, leap to the water just as the pontoon touched shore, and haul the raft aground with the nylon bowline to secure it.

One time I snubbed the line over a boulder that offered too little bite. Don sighed, got out, took the line, and retied it on a sharper chunk of rock that would afford the rope more bite if wave movement loosened the line.

"Peace of mind," he muttered, his body language signaling disapproval. We cleaned the beach by breaking apart the fire rings, flinging burnt branch ends to the water, hauling rocks off the sand, naturalizing the shore. After we finished the beach, Don also disapproved of the tautness of the loops I used to secure the bowline of the raft before I shoved the rig back into the current.

He stilled his oars and stared downstream. "Ten years ago a woman fell out and got an ankle tangled in a loose line. She was a thin gal, wearing a PFD that was cinched too loose. The boat hauled her right through the rapid. The loose jacket slid over her head. Nothing for the guide to do but cut the rope."

"Did she drown?"

"She did."

A client had tied a rope wrong, and a guide had been forced to handle a corpse. Don was offering me a narrative reproof, I understood, better anytime than an outright scolding. He told me a story by which to assess my mess-up.

We were novice volunteers on the Salmon River, visitors to what Dave Foreman has named the "Big Outside." We were very evidently not at home. We had signed release forms to work beside the uniformed veterans who spent a third of their every year on water. Dressed in our sandals and shorts, we were tourists as exotic and invasive as the spotted knapweed itself. At the end of every day, after our responsibilities fell away, we could finally loosen up.

Don's somber recollections fed my speculation about how Braden had gone down. I saw the borrowed kayak capsizing, the waves dashing it against the jagged sandstone, the desperate struggle to gain handholds and climb, the next wave drawing him back. But conjecture was unhealthy, I knew, and pointless.

The stretch of Puget Sound where he and his buddy had put in the kayaks is rocky. Sandstone makes deep tidal pools where sea otters feed. Waves lap and scoop the stone smooth. By force of suction limpets cling, those conical snails that lent their shape to Chinese hats. Predatory crabs chip at the edges of limpet shells. Crabs pry up the armored animal to expose soft flesh underneath. Sea stars, also known as starfish, some sporting more than twenty prickly limbs, use horny beaks to drill holes in snail shells and have their voracious way.

Howard Lyman is a range con, or conservationist. He mediates between the agencies and the grandee ranchers that enjoy federal generosity in the form of low grazing fees on public lands. Ranching has such a hold on the American West that some federal employees become installers of fences and troughs, guardians of fragile ecosystems against the predations of cattle. Some range cons agree to ride herd, become cowboys, to keep cows out of seedlings and water bodies.

Exotic cattle, whose earliest ancestors were domesticated in rainy Asia, tend to wade in streams, erode banks, and tug up native vegetation by the roots. A hoof-print may remain in dry-land climates for decades, because heavy cow hooves crack the stabilizing algal crusts. Running Angus and Herefords on arid soils creates conditions ideal for alien plants like spotted knapweed. Cattle, like knapweed itself, are exotic interlopers out here.

Howard finally called my bluff, after I advertised my abiding interest in native grasses and weeds. One morning at Big Mallard Creek, he lounged into camp and sat us down on a pair of precious folding chairs. He was cradling three good bunchgrasses—three indigenous plants that stabilize the soil.

"This here's prairie junegrass," he said as if introducing us formally, "Idaho fescue, and bluebunch wheatgrass." I held them and stroked the seed heads—so wispy, nodding, and frail by contrast with the spiny, seedy, forceful knapweed staining my hands. Howard worked to guard native grasses against invaders like mullein, salsify, cinquefoil, hawksbeard, and leafy spurge. When I asked him, he reamed right out the genus and species of the junegrass and fescue, but the wheatgrass cost him a thoughtful pause. "Dang taxonomists changed the name," he said, shaking his head, "but I just can't change."

Later that day Howard trudged off with a tank on his back and a spray wand in his hand. He was going after fugitive Scotch thistle. It towered eight feet high, prickly and formidable, in a camp where hunters had spread hay. I stayed well away, wary of blowback from the sprayer. He returned, face red and shirt sweaty, shed the tank and plunged into the river. The love handles above his pants, viewed from behind, looked like cheeks on a sad face.

As an officer of the federal government, Howard Lyman is charged with enforcing Executive Order 13112. Signed into law February 3, 1999, the order founded the Invasive Species Council, an organization that includes twelve White House cabinet members. Invasive species can deal serious blows to business interests. The secretaries of Agriculture, Commerce, and Interior co-chair the council. Other members include the leaders of Defense, along with the chiefs of Homeland Security, Health and Human Services, Treasury, Trade, Transportation, NASA, the EPA, and the State Department.

If pathogens are being crammed into missile heads, as U.S. generals and majors claim, nonnative species might serve hostile nations as biological weapons. What if enormous wasps were bred to stun much-larger organisms? You detect a sting, lapse into a coma, and wait—a paralyzed and immobile witness to your own doom—for the eggs attached to your abdomen to hatch. You become a vessel for a laboratory-fabricated creature that needs to eat you to survive. The late novelist Michael Crichton might have found inspiration to write about such anxieties and gotten an invitation to testify before Congress, as he did following the release of his global-warming thriller *State of Fear*.

It was suppertime on our fourth night, the sun sliding behind a hill, a couple of hours until dark. We filled our plates, sat in the sand, and watched slow dusk come on. Two prairie falcons, currents of high air made flesh, were whipping on the winds, soaring one above the other in tandem. The higher bird held a morsel of food, half a mouse by the looks of it, and dropped the morsel, passing it deftly to its mate, as if the lob had been practiced. Its partner swiveled upside down mid-flight and caught the swap without a wobble.

Wildlife flourishes in abundance in the canyon, and we were focusing on plants. Thumbing a field guide to western weeds, I was struck by what a rich book could be written about them. Prostrate pigweed, bur chervil, spiny sowthistle, blessed milkthistle, tansy ragwort, and poverty sumpweed—these plants say a lot about the Adams in Eden assigned to name them. One might stub a sandaled toe on spikeweed, hawkweed, nodding beggarticks, sagewort, gumweed, skeletonweed, wormwood, or ragweed—names dabbed on so thick they welt the throat and tongue. Or take a taste of cudweed, crupina, hawksbeard, curlycup, horseweed, fleabane, bull thistle, rabbitbrush. Such names work like vegetative imprecations, insults coughed up with scornful snorts. Skeletonleaf bursage, starthistle, toothed spurge, and puncturevine make kinds of verbal threats; they are phonetic weapons to match their leaves and thorns. Try to find affection for distaff thistle, black henbane, buffaloburr, toadflax, musk thistle, and land caltrop—a manufactured caltrop being a several-sided spiky contrivance made to wound and lame. Nature long has inspired implements of war, as when fighters armed their forts with abattis—barriers of trees whose branches had been sharpened or entwined with wire. Nature also inspires benign tools. When George de Mestral got home from a walk in Switzerland in 1948, with his spaniel covered in burrs, he looked at the embedded hooks beneath his microscope, and then he invented Velcro.

Fellow paddler Ken Kuhn pulled me from my book of weeds to tell me he had seen a pair of golden eagles team up to seize a merganser, a kind of fish-duck. The first eagle swooped. The merganser saw it and dove below the river's surface to escape its talons. Several seconds later—the instant the unwitting fish-duck surfaced—the second eagle zoomed in for the kill.

Our rangers' tales fleshed out the past and added facets to the canyon. A massive rock resembled a hippopotamus head. Stories like veins mapped the river's culture. Not only stories of people—trappers and miners, criminals and crazies, hunters and sodbusters—but also tales told by cliffs and swirling currents, high water and harsh waves, by wild animals feeding, breeding, and at play. High on a steep bank, a pair of rutting bighorn rams once sparred and plunged off ten-foot cliffs. The victor mounted the alpha ewe, made her bleat, and hopped along the trail locked on her for some time.

Constant sun that day had made me weary. The finding and the tidying, the troweling and uprooting, and the meditating on stories that marble the land had done me in. Then, too, I needed some time alone after being shoulder-to-shoulder for hours in a paddle craft. Choosing to forego the post-supper beer and conversation, I headed early to bed. On hard-packed sand beside the river current, I threw my tarp and sleeping bag as soon as it got dark. I was eager to be lulled by the swirling and gurgling of the Salmon River four feet away.

To sleep outdoors is always pacifying to me, the fresh air a narcotic. I feel safer than I do when shut inside. Such freedom from enclosure must be claustrophobia's contrary, the reverse of being made a captive in a car trunk.

At the confluence of Johnson Creek and the Salmon River, the stars so far from city lights shone in the millions. One comet shot across the entire scope of the sky. My eyes dazzled, the leaden lids slipped, and I slept hard.

Too soon, how many hours later it was hard to say, a heaving dream congealed and awoke me. I was dreaming about my lost son, his body never recovered from the depths of Puget Sound. I heard the words: *Go find your brother.* This plea, delivered in my own voice to my two young sons, sat me upright on the riverbank. I was having spasms, trembling with a familiar load of sorrow and faint faith, as if some stranger inside me still were hoping for a miracle, groping for an invincible offspring who could walk on ocean water.

In their most optimistic sense, the words *Go find your brother* might have meant: *Bring him to me, discover and rescue the one who is lost.* In the darkest recognition they cautioned: *Make the discovery of the sodden body now. Bring it home to give us closure.* My son Braden, he was gone. He had become a husk of what used to be. The Salmon River rushing past my head had melted a sac of sorrow dammed for far too long. Anxiety and its ten hands clutched me, plucked me. A grief-shell in me opened, punctured by a dream.

At that very instant, unaccountably, I recalled twin encounters with wasps many years before. In the home where I grew up, I grabbed one on a window by its wings. I pinioned it and held it for a closer view. It flexed and tried to sting, but I held tight. Soon a strong stench drifted to me. The wasp was kicking out a mighty predator repellant. On another day a wasp was flitting beneath a lawn chair, and I bent to see it transporting a ball of mud, building what looked like a honeycomb, a cartridge box, maybe a mausoleum.

I watched the wasp and waited a week before cracking open the nest beneath the chair. The cells of the nest held four spiders, two young and two adults. The juveniles were in a toxic coma or dead. The neurotoxin of the wasp had done them in. They had been too frail to stand the poison. The hardier adults, though, began to twitch. Those legless adult spiders were partially paralyzed or no longer stunned at all, their limbs severed with surgical precision. Each of them, the young and the old alike, wore a yoke-yellow saddle, an extrusion that anchored and encased the maturing wasp egg.

The adults began to pull themselves awkwardly toward the light with their pedipalps—those mouthparts males charge with sperm to inseminate the females. With the equivalent of penises, they were hauling themselves toward the light. Even more chilling, their long jaws continued to be efficient, each one tipped with a set of reddish fangs. I outweighed them by millions, they had no legs, and still they made aggressive gestures toward me.

That encounter with the wasp larvae, with the spiders encased as prey for the larvae, had been lost to me for decades.

The night was chill. Memories flooded back as I lay in my sleeping bag on that nighttime riverbank. Encounters with predators excite allegorical thinking for some religious beings. At one time I, too, felt myself inclined to draw parallels. The larva is an inner sickness, an inherited sin that gnaws. The legless spider lives as a kindly but expiring host, whose body offers up the rich food of deliverance. The female spider wasp—pure evil—had to be a stunning dominatrix. To stretch for moral lessons would be dully comforting. It would be so simple and sure.

No, I reminded myself, wasps and spiders are pieces of world we're not in charge of—parts of the planet we're not able to contain. Let them have their wild space. Eagles and falcons will rise from trees; give mute intimation that they want no part of us. Children will vanish as if swallowed by the sea. My adult son had chosen to navigate big water in a kayak without the benefit of a lifejacket. His disappearance was nothing anyone could thwart.

On the banks of the Salmon River, dawn was coming on. The few stars still visible were fading from the sky. I lay back down. My sleeping bag was wet. Heavy dew had fallen that night, but soon the sun would rise and dry it.

# Magpie in the Window

On a kitchen floor spread with newspapers, I am gutting a pumpkin. Buried to the elbow in bright flesh, stripping its innards, I scrape the hollowing carcass to make a lantern or a lamp, as so many parents before me have done. If I gut the pumpkin well, the outcome will prove spooky, the way my toddler Reed hopes it will be. He does his part by picking out the seeds. The juicy flesh and pulp have made my fingers too slippery for such work.

I hunch over, grunt as I cut, getting into it. Once Halloween has passed, we will eat this pumpkin, even though we could easily get by without it. We could purchase a pie, or cook one from a tin can packed with pureed mash. Instead we chose to grow this horse-faced jack-o-lantern from a seed then pluck it from frost-shriveled vines. We are cleaning and preparing it as we might field-dress an animal we'd raised from a suckling or killed with a bullet in a forest or a field. I grunt and thump on the pumpkin shell. It sounds wonderfully like a drum. Reed grins, shoulders in, and thumps it too.

The pumpkin's scent wafts up, an oily funk as gamy as the birds I used to hunt this time of year. The slimy seeds and strings remind me of giblets and intestines—without the blood to wash from the field jacket, or the shot to sift from the flesh when it hits our plates. The waxy white and oblong seed husks yield sweet pepitas, the meat inside the shields. We roast whole seeds with oil and sea salt until they crunch, just as I used to roast the livers and hearts of quail, pheasants, and grouse. With the pumpkin there's no worry about catching avian flu, no messy aftereffects of wounding a bird and watching it escape. Reed, a fussy feeder who often refuses meat, has eaten pumpkin seeds we've roasted in the oven before, pronouncing them as yummy as peanuts.

I wash my hands and arms in the kitchen sink. The slime and fibers, easier to cleanse than blood, slip down the sluice. I watch them swirl and remember the waste of pain that came with the killing field. Gary Snyder has a line in his poem "The Hudsonian Curlew" about three shots to get two birds: "*one went down on the water / and started to swim. / I didn't want another thing like that duck* (emphasis in original)." Decades follow the slippery filaments in the drain.

When I look up from the pumpkin, a magpie is perching outside the kitchen window. It cocks its head and gazes through the pane. I would like to say it begins springing up and down, up and down, abandoning itself to entire delight like James Wright's blue jay, confident that the branch will not break. But this is an everyday magpie, no more or less resilient than a human with a hangover. It peers at us through the kitchen glass. It flicks its lengthy tail.

The magpie would eat pumpkin seeds if given a chance, but members of its Corvidae family favor gut piles and dead flesh. They feed on carrion and road kill. Earlier this week I saw a pair of kindred starlings. They darted from a curb amid morning traffic to peck at a puddle, and then back to the curb when the traffic hurried them away. What were they doing? I slowed and leaned to see. Their attention was focused on a small pond of vomit. Some sick soul crossing the thoroughfare had puked up his meal, and it would not go to waste. Call it nature's economy. The starling rose in esteem for me just then.

When I was Reed's age, a gabbing farm wife had grabbed a rifle in her living room mid-sentence and leaned against an open door for support. She squinted through the smoke of the cigarette in her lips, squeezed the trigger, and dropped a magpie from a cherry tree, then stood the gun on its butt and took a lengthy drag. She inhaled it deep before picking up the conversation.

Her name was Laurel Kellogg. Behind her house that spring, I set my sights on capturing a magpie for a pet. Maybe I was hoping to save it from her.

Conventional wisdom said ravens, magpies, crows, and jays needed to have tongues split if the master expected them to speak. I knew I'd never have the heartlessness to slit a magpie's tongue. All I wanted was to have that iridescent plumage close at hand each day. I hankered to affiliate with the bird like a gem or jewel, to make it mine for however short a time.

The nests of magpies are messy and bulky masses of twigs in shrubs and stumpy trees. I had seen a nest in the hills every year we'd visited Dave and Laurel's ranch on Nile Creek near the tiny burg of Selah.

The time of year for catching a magpie was ideal—early in May, right when the fledglings were trying their wings. I equipped myself for the seizure of the chick as if I were Robert Frost's dire neighbor in "Mending Wall"—"Bringing a stone grasped firmly by the top / In each hand, like an old-stone savage armed." I planned my approach so I'd surprise the birds from the uphill side, forcing them to soar downhill and make my rock-toss less a chore.

With a squawk a young bird burst from the brush. It set its wings and soared downhill toward an elderberry clump. As though I were throwing a shotput, I shoved the rock in an awkward lob. The lucky toss caught the bird on the back, knocking it to the ground. There it lay, for all appearances dead.

Cradling its limp neck in one hand, body in the other, I ran to a ditch and dipped the black beak in the churning irrigation water. Its eyes opened on my looming face, imprinted upon me, I suppose. I toted it home in a box.

Despite braining it that way, I cared for that bird with every tender attention. It grew to know me, came to my finger, and rode on the back of my mongrel dog. It flew like a falcon to capture dragonflies, trapped in the garage and dashing themselves against the picture window. Despite my loving care, each year when leaf-fall comes I suffer the impulse to take up my small armory of inherited rifles and shotguns, imprinted as I have been by Laurel Kellogg and my father to drop birds from high perches and from the air.

I call Reed to the kitchen window and point out the magpie. He runs and fetches his short kitchen stool, climbs atop it, gawks at the bird, and asks if we should offer it some bread. He confuses the ducks in Manito Park and the gulls at Lake Pend Oreille with this bird that would be too wary, wise, self-sufficient, and wild to accept handouts. I say to Reed that I once had a magpie as a pet, and he wants more details. In his world, lived stories are better than invented stories any day, and the best of all are those that involve hunting, weapons, animals, or birds. I hold my fire until bedtime, when tales of long ago have come to be expected by custom, culture, and convention.

Some day Reed might aspire to take up arms against a flock of birds and fell one. Some day he might have a trigger-happy child of his own to tutor in the ins and outs of rifles and scatterguns. I decide to take him next month to a killing field where the laws are liberal, where deer are thick and hunters flock to put venison in the pot. He might hear some gunshots and see gut heaps. In late November, the innards lie lumped in every brushy draw. "Either sex," the game laws say, and so the six-month yearlings, the does and button bucks and spikes, each relinquish a bushel-full of entrails more or less.

He will see exactly what makes a mule deer tick. He will want to inspect it all. He will be tempted to pick up a stick to poke around among the clots of spongy lungs and intestine ropes. The blood-stained snow, the drag marks and flat grass, will make a splash more vivid for him than a collection of snapshots from *Field and Stream* he browses with me in an auto-repair shop lobby. In that brushy draw of Mink Creek I won't withhold from him his first whiff of burnt gunpowder, or the sound of a wounded deer bleating like a lamb.

Together we will hike along the draw and flush scattered flocks of magpies from their frozen feasts. We will wonder how they manage it in the frigid late-November weather, how the birds make do to loosen mouthfuls from such unwieldy bladders, such icy lumps of frozen fat and flesh. The junipers will gleam and the sagebrush will be shagged with frost. The tails of the magpies, like so many comets, will stream behind them as they flee us.

When he hits adolescence I might take him to participate in a dove hunt. If the migratory birds are plentiful that year, and if hunters have yet to break up the flocks, slender mourning doves will hurtle from every direction, feinting and dodging the shot shells exploding below. Singles, pairs, flocks of dozens—hollow bones and the rapid slice of feathers overhead. I will not carry a gun in that field, but I will give Reed the youth-model 20-gauge I got for Christmas when I was twelve, with its short barrel and softie recoil pad.

Rows of hunters will hear wings whistle near. The men will have come across the Cascades for some shirtsleeve fun in the fields of wheat, many of them already partying and red-faced, unaccustomed to the mountain sun. From a bird's-eye view the shotgun barrels will rise like broomsticks, swing along the twisting line of bird-flight and past it, scattering lead shot as if making a celebration or salute. Pellets will shower the poplar leaves. About that time I will get nervous about the lack of caution my fellow hunters betray, and I will seek for Reed a vantage point some distance from the mayhem. I will tell him about a friend who got a shotgun pellet lodged in his eye for life.

Beer-silly and shouting, perched on straw bales or folding camp stools they've brought along, the hunters will wave across wheat fields at buddies, chase gun-shy dogs, they will cuff those dogs that won't fetch birds. Birds the size of thrushes, only sand-gray and sleeker, with barred and pointed tails. Doves rarely die outright, but instead release a puff of feathers and angle down like fighter planes, nosedive and hurtle in rough fluttering cartwheels, arch-necked, until hunters catch up and crush the skulls or wring the necks.

Autumn is the time of year I get ambitious to instruct my son. I want to take him away from our cautious kitchen where a pumpkin is as wild as it gets. I want to get him out of the house, away from the movies and video games that make everything else a bore. I want so many things for him, but language is chiefly what he gets—poems and stories at bedtime. One of those recitals is by Howard Nemerov, a poem entitled "The Distances They Keep."

Whenever I tell my boys the poem, I think about when I saw Nemerov give a reading not long before he died, his head closely crew-cut, his bearing almost military. It is a poem of praise for those species of birds that "have the wit to stay away." The avian occupants of Nemerov's imagination "show no desire to become our friends." The magpie in the window must be sharp enough to know that birds of this cold world do well to keep their distance.

Maybe I will take Reed to Inkom, by way of Hoot Owl and Buck-skin, to help him lay claim to place names so plain each weighs like a homely pebble under the tongue. One lies smooth and useful as obsidian, a tool lashed fast on poles and thrown toward antelope pounding along a path from the peak. Another's gnarly and jagged, a lava bubble popped when great heat melted it to grease then cooled off. A third's neither beautiful nor approved by age but fixed stubborn as a beast that brays from the aspen patch now shedding its leaves. A blind man would know where he was to hear the magpies yammer and demand the hawthorns back. Dad's tripping out again, Reed will nod, when Mom pokes her head in the bedroom and suggests we curtail the talk.

Reed's Grandma Dee might object to our jags, as much as she objects to the motorcycles I eye every spring and vow to buy. Her displeasure makes our would-be journeys more alluring. A high Victorian window will frame her face as we purr off on a full-dress Gold Wing for Lolo Hot Springs. She would like to imagine the provinces forever swaddled in Latin, bathed in Greek, fed by French cuisine. We notify her that the rock-hard names remain.

Portneuf crumbles to sand grains, and wind sweeps Montpelier bare as basalt. Stones we strike along on our pathway yield up sweet drink. Apples drop about our heads, asparagus buds split stone crevices overnight, and horned larks rise in stiff flocks everywhere from sage.

Out of the earth's odd corners blow tons of blossoms. There we'll swing along full autumn limbs the orchard reaches to our hands. Praise is a language tough to separate from love, I will assure my son. If owls hoot, onomatopoeia calls it grief. And *coeurs*, in the sandy backward paths we will travel, is chiefly an angry oath.

Sometimes I think Reed goes along on my word journeys and land travels just to humor me. Afloat in the dark on the tide of language that rises from my lips, he might be turning to his schoolwork, to a new film he saw, to cueing up a YouTube video, or hatching a vengeful adolescence. He knows how often I find myself flocking on far horizons with the earnest birds of passage.

The magpie in the window flicks its tail. It fluffs its feathers, unrolls its wings, and gives up on us. It launches from the pine branch like a diver coming off a board. Or, like lone shoulders in a rowboat, the bird plies its oars just enough to take it into the next pine, the next yard, the next human prospect.

The pumpkin is done and it's time for bed. We gather up the edges of the newspapers on the floor and fold them for the compost. Place a candle in the jack-o-lantern's hollow, reach a match in a nostril to light the wick. On the porch it will burn for hours, sending up a scent of gently scorching flesh.

# Genius Loci

The abiding spirits of ponderosa forests take the form of humble nuthatches. If the wind isn't sifting too loudly through the pine needles, if the local ravens aren't being raucous, you may hear them. Their call will float, a nasal horning, neither peep nor squawk nor squeak. It is a tone most like the tedious beep of a work truck backing up. Red-breasted, white-breasted, pygmy nuthatches—these are genius loci. One may lay hands on them all, though making captives of wild birds always risks some harm. To grasp a one-ounce nuthatch, whose habits evolved with western pines, will cause its heart to beat hazardously fast. Nuthatches are external talents of the trees, elusive ghosts of their homes.

Upside down they creep, beaking off bark flecks, tossing them to earth. In ways that science and metaphysics both may claim, nuthatches groom the trees, tending to them as pilot fish tend to a whale. The bond is symbiotic.

In summer they favor the same beetles, wasps, spiders, and flies that lay eggs, drill holes, harbor beneath the bark, and ravage ponderosa cones. Nuthatches vault to hawk or snatch up airborne bugs. Come winter, they tweezer nuts from pinecones with their bills, wedge them in cracks and crevices of bark or stone, and use their heads as hammers to hatchet or hatch them open. The word *hatch* derives from the dialectic drift of English colonists. These small birds care for forests of large trees.

Rest beneath their sturdy vigor and you will bathe in scraps of bark resembling jigsaw-puzzle pieces, as my boys and I did one spring day. We lay in the yard and gazed straight up to the heights where gargantuan ponderosa pine trunks and their branches got well groomed. The bark chips fell around us. The shards showered down.

Lounging with Reed and Chase beneath the pines was peaceful, but I should have been refurbishing our old house. It needed lots of work. After years of renting, Karen and I had bought this big frame dwelling, on the margin between the urban and the rural, between the wild and the tame, in a neighborhood where turkeys, moose, coyotes, and mule deer feed, breed, and migrate through.

That old house cried out for loving justice. Rain and snow had warped the shiplap cedar siding in spots. To the west and to the south, blazing sun had flaked the stain. Beneath the eaves, where wire mesh is meant to ventilate air in the attic, the screens had crumpled and bent, giving refuge to birds and bugs. The eaves furnished a perfect location for making nests — the space was warm, shady, quiet, and dry.

To begin to mend the screens in the eaves, I hauled a stepladder up to the study and had Karen steady it. I climbed up three rungs, pushed open a ceiling hatch, and laid it aside. I moved a broom and flashlight into that dim space. Climbing two more steps, I thrust my head inside the attic. Peering at floor level made me edgy, as I was infringing on the spaces claimed by birds, bugs, bats, or mice. The gloom lay thickest at the peak of the roof, but eaves admitting light alleviated it below. I rested my elbows on either side of the narrow opening to the attic, and Karen went back to her paperwork.

Her legal career had taken an urgent turn in recent weeks. She sued a group of farmers for polluting the skies of northern Idaho and Spokane. Working for her client, the nonprofit group Safe Air for Everyone, Karen had forced the farmers to comply with the Americans with Disabilities Act of 1990 and stop burning stubble with such reckless disregard. Respiratory disease and death accompanied the smoke from their bluegrass fields.

One night our house had been vandalized, a reprisal that draped the eaves and trees with twenty-four rolls of toilet paper. Her Subaru in the driveway had been papered, too, that paper soaked in piss. The defacement was meant to convey a message: *We know where you live.* My courageous wife, never one to back down from a fight, had carried on against all odds, showing me the spirit that earned her state swimming awards in her teens.

Months after the vandalism, though, something else still troubled me about the house. Above the city lights it seemed to lean, on a knoll that made me feel susceptible, as if we all might slip off the cliff, flip into space. Wind whooped and screeched through the trees, stern enough to rip off roof tiles during one long night. Superstition like a grizzled guard dog stalked the yard, and I procrastinated at the task of chasing it away. Pine branches and needles hackled at every eave and pane. The night skies forced upon me a form of agoraphobia, and beneath the winter star-glare I felt searched and seized.

Our aging house disturbed me because the former owner had taken his life. Some taboo makes suicide tough to discuss, as if one were sharing family secrets or betraying the dead.

Gentle and upbeat by all reports, the previous owner, Richard, had papered the indoors of the house in clashing patterns. He had planted pastel flowers in stone-edged beds. He took to tending an empty lot far down the street, a hot patch of rocks and wildflowers that is sure to be bulldozed sooner or later. There he planted sprawling squash vines and hauled gallons of water, even though a garden plot in his own backyard had sprinkler heads plumbed in.

When he turned up dead, his neighbors, our neighbors now, were shocked. Just after 8:00 AM his twelve-year-old daughter found him on her way to school. The automatic garage door had been made to gape all day, his body beneath the receiver on the ceiling, the detectives doing their research to uncover any signs of foul play. Casual passersby and children off the bus could view the tranquility he had labored hard for.

Below his jawbone the pistol slug came in, exiting his left temple. He had planned his own end well. But why, I kept wondering, undo himself and his family where his daughter would make the find?

No stranger to suicide, I have forebears on both sides who took their lives — both of them males, both with handguns. We never had a chance to meet. Worrying over the Depression, my mother's father shot himself in their Seattle kitchen. My mom and her siblings had to quit school and find jobs to help their widowed mother. Then, a decade later, one of my two paternal uncles came home from World War II with a plate in his head. He found his lover in love with another. Outside a Seattle café my uncle and his former sweetheart quarreled. When she ran for help, he chased her through the building and shot her, afterward turning the gun on himself in a public murder-suicide. My father, a teenager, could not bear to venture out of the house for weeks.

When I was an adolescent I felt ancient already, as if I had "sampled all that springs to birth / from the many-venomed earth," as A. E. Housman wrote. Some dark poems of mine fell into the hands of my parents, who took me to see a minister, then later a physician. Both recommended writing about one's troubles as a splendid way to open them to light and air.

Since then I have come to believe that suicide and laughter, our low and our high moods both, distinguish us from other species like few other behaviors, divide us from the other mammals on this planet. Anxious people will die. On the other hand, I do not mind taking cues from so-called lower animals, whose simpler natures seem so often to afford them better sense.

The rumors said Richard's ex-wife had given him a hard time about the kids. She had "taken her feminism down a recreational path," the rumors said, fallen in love with another woman. She had *gone lesbian*—as if to say she had gone feral. She spirited away the younger three of the five children with her when she went. As a psychiatrist, his ex-wife really knew how to push Richard's buttons, or so the grapevine said. He turned to pharmaceuticals, but his physicians got the doses wrong or mixed and matched them in bad ways. Malpractice allegations were swirling. Someone was going to get sued.

We met Richard's widow, a woman fragile as a cracker on a mattress. With the loss of Richard's income, she needed to sell the house. Her realtor, Sheila, wore red nails, high heels, lavish makeup, and a studio tan. When a suicide has occurred in a dwelling, state laws mandate the event must be disclosed to every potential buyer. Guiding us through the house, stepping into the garage, Sheila tossed her sable mane and sprung the story on us at that moment. She said we shouldn't worry, though; the insurance company had paid to repaint the space. The consolation of philosophy, so at odds with commerce today, seemed downright quaint just then. The world is "seared with trade, bleared and smeared with toil," the poet Gerard Manley Hopkins wrote.

We bought the house, but before moving in we worked some American Indian cures. We smudged with sage sticks and sweet grass. We slapped and shouted in every corner and hall. As the first place to make over, I chose the garage floor, scrubbing up dog residues and secret stains, patching spidery cracks with putty. Bending and coating that floor, a picture of a humble laborer on my knees, I mumbled some verses on behalf of Richard and his estranged ex-wife, his widow and all of his children, and my own family as well.

A year after Richard died, nuthatches began to hammer on the outer walls. Soft spots and loose knots invited them to pound and peck, prod and wedge, seeking bugs for food and cavities for nests. To perplex their pecking, I filled the growing holes with a resin too resistant to punch through. I knew I was spurning genius loci, thwarting them for the time being, though above one high deck I hung a heavy swag of a feeder and filled it with sunflower seeds.

Songbirds began smashing into our big windows. The far-off space they thought they saw was light reflected from behind them. They fell to the deck and grew stiff. Most juncos, nuthatches, sparrows, and finches survived after hitting a window, but the larger crossbills, robins, flickers, and quail were apt to die, their necks broken by the blow. Most of those unlucky fliers left behind them reminders of their collisions. Feathers, plastered on the glass, fluttered there. To turn the birds away, I stuck one of Chase's dolls to a window by the suction cups of its palms. Birds set to smack the pane began to slow or veer. To make the other windows more visible, I fastened sticky notes.

Birds congregating at feeders, I learned, exchange germs and furnish hunting grounds for snakes, hawks, and housecats. Cats kill some thirty million songbirds every year in North America alone. Twice-hapless birds might hit a window, tumble unconscious to the ground, and then get plucked. In the Sonoran Desert I saw a roadrunner snatch and swallow whole a warbler stunned beneath a picture window. There, too, a sharp-shinned hawk swooped on a feeder and scattered songbirds everywhere — into windows, into walls — hoping for a slow stray. Falcons, in our busiest city park in Spokane, pester crows for spite or fun, driving them from the breadcrumbs thrown to ducks at the pond, chasing the usually boisterous crows from tree to tree in hostile joy.

Winged migration puzzled early naturalists, who guessed that "birds of passage" overwintered underwater or hibernated in caves like bears. A scrap of truth might have nestled in that wild surmise. Most species of nuthatches, like crows, never migrate. They tough out the savage northerly winters, holing up in any cavity they can find, clustering in tree trunks or basalt breaks, a hundred bodies huddled together, all gone hypothermic. They have a knack for withstanding cold.

We warmer humans migrate likewise. Place after place, job following job, we rent houses and build houses or shift into old ones, sleeping in the same stale rooms as prior tenants, breathing in their confined air, cracking eggs over the same gray stoves for decades. Concentration and confinement taint us like so many germs. When worries thrill us beyond endurance, we pack up and flee. I am still learning how to stay in one place and connect with it, how to cohabit with other beings that find their habitations there.

Maybe genius loci were cooping in our attic. It was too dark to see. My eyes were beginning to widen in the dark, but the flashlight had rolled out of reach. Karen was clacking away at her keyboard below, wondering what was taking me so long, but in her fond and tolerant way never bothering to ask.

Ornithologists report that nuthatches "maintain a long-term pair bond," a relationship that differs precisely from mating for life. Actual monogamy, as the evolutionary biologist Olivia Judson writes, is rare. "So rare that it is one of the most deviant behaviors in biology." Older male nuthatch offspring help their parents build and look after nests. They feed and guard the mother and younger siblings once they hatch. They form units in an extended family that helps to perpetuate their particular strands of DNA.

When we first got together, I alarmed Karen by giving my rank opinion that humans tend toward serial monogamy only, that real permanence proves elusive. Now here we were, a dozen years and two children later, still growing within one another's expanding boundaries, building a long-term pair bond.

To defend and extend nuthatch families, the parents and their helpers perform a kind of dooryard voodoo. They construct sap traps. To do so, they coat the entryways of their nesting cavities with pine, fir, or spruce pitch. Intruders—birds or mammals, reptiles or bugs—become ensnared there. Adult nuthatches, shaped much like torpedoes, rocket through the jiggered entryways to keep from getting stuck, though one watcher did discover a nuthatch dead at its door, worn out from struggling, mired by its own device.

Another form of nest defense sets nuthatches apart. They practice bill sweeping. Seizing smelly ants or blister beetles that secrete chemical irritants, they brush and sweep the perimeters of their nests. Evidence suggests the chemicals in the insects repel predatory mammals or birds. The beetles exude a drug that produces blisters; ants emit a formic acid vapor when disturbed.

Some jays bathe in the tiny streams of acid that ants spray when they are seized and under stress, a practice that has given rise to the coinage *anting*. The acid evidently does not affect the bather, but it drives away lice or mites on the feathers of the birds. Nuthatches tend to breed in cracks and cavities, as do the same ants, wasps, and beetles that have been known to swarm and kill hatchlings. Bees and nettles likewise emit strong formic acid.

By daubing conifer pitch on doorways, by smearing stinky bugs, nuthatches might be warding off predatory insects, or so I surmised from my attic height. If featherless nestlings stung to death by insects prove gruesome for the human viewer, they must be all the more so for the nuthatch parents.

In his brilliant book *On Watching Birds*, Lawrence Kilham writes of a white-breasted nuthatch that behaved as if possessed while it engaged itself in sweeping. Kilham could hear the manic swishing from more than sixty feet away. A watcher in my home might have found my own actions somewhat manic — painting the garage floor, patching holes in the siding, now nerving up myself to ascend into the attic space.

Molecular studies, adjusting everything we know about speciation, have linked nuthatches with the corvids — ravens, crows, magpies, jays, and nutcrackers. Nuthatches and nutcrackers make their livings in the same trees as these other birds. And, it turns out, they stem from the same genetic trunk.

Nuthatches specialized, though. They developed long hind toes like the woodpeckers and learned to creep down conifer trunks instead of up. This head-down advance, allowing them to see food from above as well as below, proved to be an adaptive breakthrough, an evolutionary advantage. The birds with the longest hind toes survived to reproduce and pass on those genes. Then, too, the light-colored throats and breasts of nuthatches reflect valuable light to illumine cracks in the corrugated bark of ponderosa pines and firs.

Nuthatches have eyesight keen as magpies and crows, whose curiosity is legendary. Like the other corvids, too, nuthatches roost communally and overwinter in cold climes. What is more, like their truly omnivorous cousins the magpies and crows, nuthatches sometimes amass food and glean tidbits from carrion—maggots mostly, one might guess, though over time the nuthatch species may well develop a kindred taste for dead flesh.

Foretelling Poe's metronome of a poem entitled "The Raven," colonists to the North American continent dubbed the humble nuthatch "devil-down-head," a kenning that says how far this minuscule hoarder of seeds, these genius loci with their horning cry, have grown estranged from humankind.

The attic I was entering to clean was cool. It was a far cry from the garage, on the opposite side of the house and two floors higher. How loud must the shot from the garage have sounded from that distance? I shoved my shoulders through the narrow hatch, as if I were rehearsing my own birth. My mother Juanita, dwelling solo since my father died, might have rejected the parallel.

My own family had occupied the house less than a year. Though the title held our name, the structure still resisted us somehow, as if it were animated by both sentience and will. One set of neighbors, Richard's closest friends, seemed unwilling to relinquish the house to us after Richard's widow sold. They appeared resentful of our sudden advent. Their behavior toward us said we should have asked them first, should have gained a neighborhood plebiscite before we moved in. Interlopers, intruders, pests. Cool and silent, the shifting edges of those mysteries lingered in the air where a father and a husband had lived and labored, planted and wallpapered, fretted and died.

The dust in the attic made me snuff. What was I inhaling, I wondered. Every breath we take contains thousands of carbon particles from formerly warm lives. Other beings, most of them long dead, have shed cells of flesh that we are taking in. Prince Hamlet, on the edge of lunacy, taunts his murderous uncle, King Claudius, with the observation that "a man may fish with a worm that hath eat of a king, and eat of the fish that hath fed of that worm." His purpose: to show "how a king may go a progress through the guts of a beggar."

In ways it is hard to fix a name to, the same applies to all domestic space. A man or woman may sleep in a room where a madman has slept and may breathe the dander his family shed. In a scene from the John Sayles film *Brother from Another Planet*, the extrasensory-perceptive alien who crashes to planet Earth sits on an Ellis Island bench, but suffers a start when he hears the cries of immigrants there before him. The ancient Romans worshiped a domestic god by the name of Lares; it presided over households and estates.

Outside our attic, ponderosa pines grow straight from cracks in basalt. The trees give homes to nuthatches, ravens, nutcrackers, and crows. The tree roots broaden holes and fissures, admit leaves and dust and blown topsoil, building humus as they do. The igneous stone basalt, molten millions of years ago, displays tiny dimples where gas bubbles hissed, textures that furnish purchase when nuthatches search the cavities and cracks for nests and food.

Basalt arose from fissures as magma, it liquefied Earth's crust, it broke through as lava to spread across the land so long ago. When the lava cooled, its scattering gases pocked the rock. Basalt in some places descends three full miles below the planet's surface on the Columbia Plateau where we live. When the magma cooled unrestricted by pressure from surrounding stone, basalt crystallized as rows of massive hexagonal columns prized by rock hounds.

Grand slabs of basalt — split along columnar cracks, loaded by cranes, transported in flatbed trucks — augment posh boulevards and furnish support for mailboxes. They make for pretty ornaments. Basalt also is being plundered from public lands, stolen by rock rustlers, lifted by landscape thieves, spirited away by those who would take the whole world to do with as they see fit.

Lichens of many species colonize the basalt and cover it in technicolor patches of green, blue, yellow, orange, or red. Rock surfaces, whole hillsides, become the color of the lichens that most take hold. At nearby Williams Lake, basalt columns fall to the shore from hillsides on the shoreline and show a smoldering ochre, a brownish red that glows as if the stone itself were aflame. Diners gazing from the windows or the deck of the restaurant there may watch the colonnades of basalt darkly blaze.

Lichen contains twin organisms enfolded in a symbiotic clutch — the first a kind of fungus, the second a kind of alga. The algae benefit the fungi, which do not possess any chlorophyll and thus cannot photosynthesize food. The lichen's algal part feeds its fungal part.

The fungi benefit the algae in turn by finding and absorbing nutrients and water. Lichen clusters get plucked by the nuthatches, hauled and stuffed in stones with nervous care, serving birds as a wadding to keep their surplus seeds and kernels crammed in basalt cracks.

Wavering in the attic crawl space, breathing in past lives, I admitted to myself that I was stalling, brooding. I knew I needed to excavate the junk, face the task however nasty, swing a broom and topple some things. It was far past time to get to work. I located the heavy steel flashlight made for use by cops. Creeping off the ladder rungs, I reached it, switched it on, stood straight up.

The bent screens came into view, the decrepit bird nests, the frayed and straying insulation, the bat guano, and the paper wasp hives. Fingering one fallen hive, I saw that stillborn wasp pupas still clogged some of the cells.

From one crevice I lifted a bird nest, knowing it was an old one dating to well before nesting season, worrying all the same that genius loci might yet be tenanting there. Grass, feathers, and human hair lined the twig shell of the nest—dead growths that had been gathered by the nest builders with care, borne by beaks full, woven into place. And on the floor, crumbled, a fragment of an eggshell appeared, creamy with brown specks. A chick of some small bird had hatched there, had shoved its shoulders through the shards.

The nest lay loose in my hand, the inner softness of its lining straying from the harder outer husk. When I turned the nest over, from it fluttered something dried and dense like dung, but plumed. The plumed clod made a muffled click on the floor. I squatted and plucked it up between two fingers.

In my palm it lay—a one-inch blob, gray and oblong. Holding it closer to the flashlight lens, I played the light across it. At first the clod looked like a plumb bob—a tool often used to measure watery depths—but it tapered to a point from which a tiny curving feather stemmed. It was a feather so fine that it might have been an eyelash, a watercolorist's brush, maybe the delicate cilia that a barnacle will unfurl to filter seawater for food.

Maybe some mammal had denned in our eaves, I reasoned, had swallowed a feather and left this chunk of dung. Its hazy lines grew more distinct. Where the fine quill vanished, a chain emerged, a string of minute vertebrae, then a beak encircling the shaft of the quill. That was the point I recognized it—the hatchling legs clenched and curled like hairs, the bulbous eyes screwed shut. I stood up in the attic and suffered an intense head rush.

The previous night I had lain awake and made a mental list of chores to be done. Now I held a husk that supported life only a few hours, a hatchling bird that had died under this same roof. It captivated me, the plumed clod. As if relishing my own gooseflesh, I tried to imagine how it had come to take that exotic shape. The blind mouth must have groped toward light, felt as if light nourished it. Straining and clacking until light paused to stuff it, peeping faintly, it had wrongly gulped the plume used by its tender parent to soften the nest.

Halfway down its throat that errant feather from another species went, until light ceased and hunger also fled. So this is the way faint songs subside. In my palm it lay—rigid, insensible, a pinch away from productive dust.

On the outer wall of the house a nuthatch hammered, as if summoning me to open a locked door. All of a sudden I needed brighter light and purer air. At once I found the attic too confining. I felt woozy and wanted to escape, needed to get away. But with a combination of grief and relief I acknowledged to myself that there is no away, that the death of this hatchling was playing out across the planet a thousand times in the instant it took me to blink, and that our old home's last owner had exercised the same free will we all enjoy.

Light filtered through the vents and the crumpled screens. I sat down, expelled some breath, peered out beneath the eaves. Swallows had flown from Mexico and were skimming the lawn to pick up airborne bugs. Soon they would be quarrelling with protective nuthatches to nest in these same eaves.

I needed to drag away the cobwebs, repair or replace the screens, and return downstairs to my desk cluttered with papers and other odd objects—a glass with an inch of cloudy water, photos of my family at play in Lake Pend Oreille, and a book by Thomas Berry entitled *The Dream of the Earth*.

Four months later I held a nuthatch in my hand. It had banged against a window on a cabin where I was a guest. I heard the impact and found the bird on the ground. Maybe it wasn't dead, I reasoned. Maybe I could help to save these genius loci before sprawl had fully paved the way. Then, too, I worried some predator might gobble the inert bird before it could come around.

And so I gathered up its body—I did, me—always a sucker for a songbird close at hand. I turned it over, admired its bullet shape, and fell under the spell of its sensuous self. Then I slipped it in my jacket pocket and had some lunch. It nestled snug beside my liver, torpid there but warm.

Some might find the impulse grisly, to make a keepsake of a corpse. Some might regard human remains as husks to watch over once the sacred souls have flown. I do not. In the cycle that keeps organic systems sound, the body and its substance must be the stuff of love itself. If you have to pray—I should like to interrupt my own memorial service to say—advocate for the conversion of my earthly carcass. Please help these precious cells take flight.

Ponderosa pines vaulted from the basalt. They soared toward the July sky as if to shield my family from the winter winds that blew so rude. Driving downhill, growing lightheaded from the altitude change, I made the short trip home. Pine pollen and road dust rose in plumes behind the Honda wagon.

As I neared the old house with the shiplap siding, the nuthatch I had jacketed beside my liver began to twitch. It shoved its beak and shoulders to discover some way out. Reaching in to release it, one hand on the wheel, I fumbled, all thumbs, and the bird escaped inside the car. It saw sheltering trees beyond the windowed confines, but it found only rigid glass to smack.

In the driveway I ground the car to a halt and wound all four windows down. At the rear of the wagon the bird scurried, as far from me as it could get. I could have opened the hatch. Instead I crawled on the cramped back seat and hustled with my hands to make it mine, examined its beak for blood, and admired it all over again. I opened my hand, palm up, and the nuthatch beelined for a pine. There it sat, shook its head, and squinted at the sun.

Still today, on the wall outside the study Karen and I share, nuthatches prod and wedge, pound and peck. They cannot be stopped. Inside our walls, dwelling neither within our house nor exactly outside, they soak up some of the warmth that radiates from our living space. I never patch the holes they bore anymore. What for, when they would only gouge them again?

Disparate species, we are learning to coexist, each of us growing on the other. The horning cries of nuthatches drift over our neighborhood rooftops. The tiles beneath the chimney on the roof of our house lift in winter winds, the cedar siding curls and warps, and the pine trees sway overhead, their needles hackling, cones and birds together plunging when the branches lash.

# Subliming the System

*The days close to winter*
*Rough with strong sound. We hear the sea and the forest.*
— *Louise Bogan*

To shovel is to shove when it comes to snow. We try to heap snow until it melts. We want to keep from packing it hard with our shoes or tires. We try to keep from turning it to ice. One night last winter, heavy snow began falling at dusk and no one in our household had the spunk to get outside and shove it. All our best intentions went to bed and the snow fell in heaps—on the steps, on the driveway, in the yard, and on the street. I set an alarm to rise before dawn and set about the job of grunting down the driveway with a deep snow shovel.

Sometime in the middle of the night a wind kicked up. It woke me first. Karen lay curled beside me with her hands between her knees. Wind ravaged the pines and tossed around odd objects on porches and decks. Finally it woke her. We listened from the bed, her hand caught carefully inside mine. The wind toppled the garbage can and the recycle bins. It scattered cardboard and tin cans. Newspapers flapped across the yard like bats. It sounded as if a full-tilt blizzard had blown in. Several weeks earlier, a neighbor's tree had crashed through the roof of his house, a story that made us fret about our own home, surrounded by gigantic ponderosa pines. Surely the snow was piling up. Surely we would wake to a heavy mantle so common in our northerly home.

The next morning we looked out to find that new snow gone. Maybe the wind had been powerful enough to drift the flakes against a fence, down the hill, across the street. But no: when I went to gather the trash and puzzle past the mystery, the snow was gone. A warm wind was blowing; the winter felt like spring. A Chinook wind had sublimed the snow—turned it to a gas without liquefying it. The wind gasified the snow and lifted it to the clouds.

All week I tried to reconcile that meteorological event with the concept of the sublime as nineteenth-century American painters used and knew it. Thomas Cole, Frederic Edwin Church, Thomas Moran, and Albert Bierstadt made canvases so illuminated by awe they seem to be depicting heaven. Those Hudson River School painters created scenery imbued with "a greatness with which nothing else may be compared," or so one of their commentators said.

Those landscape paintings—lavish with shafts of golden light, purple mountains, hooded clouds, and human lookers stunned to silence—inscribe the presence of God. Taking shorthand for divinity, the painters aimed to translate sacred landscapes for lay viewers. Self-ordained, they mediated between the lord, the land, and the laity.

No sooner had our late evening snow fallen than it was gone. So, too, moments of divine insight had to be captured fast when devout painters witnessed them firsthand. A prudent deity never allows His finest works to turn to liquid before subsuming them back to the sky; making this mortal coil too appealing would be wrong. The planet Earth is meant to be comprehended less as a place for making pleasure in the here-and-now than as a replica of heaven, a kiss and a promise to be consummated only in the afterlife.

Grand Coulee Dam, built by the Bureau of Reclamation during World War II, outstrips every other concrete structure in North America for its massive scale. It also thwarts migrating native salmon from hundreds of miles of ideal spawning grounds upstream. The tribal people who relied on those fish lost a legacy they still feel today.

In the 1960s the U.S. federal government played god by enlisting painters to celebrate its altered landscapes. It hired painters to glorify dammed lands. So many citizens had begun to criticize dams the fed had built—so much precious PR had been lost—the bureaucrats reasoned art should be drafted to ride in to the rescue. It had worked decades earlier when singer Woody Guthrie signed a contract to write songs about dams. Such stirring tunes as "Roll On, Columbia" had celebrated plugged-up western rivers as if they still were running free. It was a minor miracle the father of Arlo Guthrie managed to discover inspiration enough in federal dams to write a song a day for thirty consecutive days. Artistic propaganda worked again in the early 1960s when NASA commissioned a series of fine art works.

Grand Coulee lies in my bioregion. I travel past it whenever no other route affords. I remember Colville and Spokane Indians praying one spring—when the Columbia River upstream from the dam was running strong—for the salmon to return. Sometimes, in my own faint way, I pause beside the water and say a few words to propitiate the salmon. My friends think I'm crazy.

To make Grand Coulee striking today as well as functional, the U. S. government screens movies and laser light shows on the mammoth concrete dam face. The art of cinematic projection might make some of the comers to that steep-sided ravine feel better about the fact that the agency drew to a halt the grandest river in the vast Pacific Northwest. The handsome laser light, projected on the dam like a movie screen, aims to camouflage the losses of salmon and cultural resources suffered by the Indian tribes.

A division of the Department of the Interior, which manages public lands, the Bureau of Reclamation was under mounting pressure in the 1960s. Americans had made advances in environmental literacy and were regarding with a jaded gaze the tens of thousands of major dams erected out west since the agency was founded at the turn of the century. After the passage of landmark legislation—the Wilderness Act of 1964, the Wild and Scenic Rivers Act of 1968, and the National Environmental Policy Act of 1969—the Bureau of Reclamation found itself on the defensive.

High dams like Grand Coulee serve passably well as monuments to empire. As icons, they trigger in me a kind of culture cringe. While others may believe that ours is an exemplary nation destined to greatness and chosen by God, I just cringe. The dams in the Pacific Northwest make me feel ashamed. When I visited the Notre Dame Cathedral in Paris, I felt a rush of loss at realizing that America's grandest edifices had been erected not for the reverence of deity, but as tombstones to the largest rivers in the American West.

Glen Canyon Dam in Arizona fueled the writer Edward Abbey in his abhorrence of industrial capitalism. Its dam gates opened in 1963. His novel *The Monkey-Wrench Gang* fantasizes about blowing up Glen Canyon. That dam also fueled the fury of the group Earth First! that

Abbey helped to found. When Earth First! went public, one historian wrote, they "chose the dam at Glen Canyon for their stage. From the top of that dam face, they unfurled a three-hundred-foot ribbon of black polyethylene tapered at the bottom to resemble a crack." Photos of that caper ran in newspapers across the nation, inspiring closeted and mainstream environmentalists alike to mount more daring acts of protest, guerilla-theater, and property sabotage.

To peg the supposed communist Woody Guthrie as a proxy for empire is apt to catch his earnest fans off guard. His guitar, fans will be fast to remind his attackers, bore the longhand slogan, "This machine kills fascists." Guthrie might not have recognized that he was being made a shill for government expansion and technology. He was hungry. He was poor. Maybe he believed, like Karl Marx had believed some eighty years before him, that technology would help to bring about the liberation of working classes around the globe.

More than forty years after Woody Guthrie, some of the paintings commissioned by Reclamation still beguile us in the ways they use visual arts to disguise the ecological damage. We might call it the fine art of bureaucracy.

*Night—Grand Coulee*, a large oil painting on canvas by government-art veteran Mitchell Jamieson, shows off the dam like a brightly lighted Parisian stage spectacle. It applies the magenta colors and the stippling technique of painting known as pointillism. It dazzles. Jamieson's *Grand Coulee* canvas invites viewers to appreciate the dam as a kind of earthly constellation, made by humans, equal to the otherworldly wonder of the stars.

Another veteran of government art, Anton Refregier, a Russian immigrant, also focused on Grand Coulee. His pastel, *Builders at Grand Coulee Dam—No. 9*, taps into the social realist interests and the propaganda aesthetics that typify the Great Depression. Refregier's faceless welders team up to exert brawny mastery over the Columbia River. They are worker bees, replicas of one another, exerting boundless energy for the collective good.

Maybe the most imaginative depiction of Grand Coulee is *Inside the Turbine*. The eerie lighting of that oil-on-canvas piece by Fletcher Martin, who taught art at a number of colleges, including nearby Washington State University, makes the turbine appear to be a piece of human anatomy, a cavity in which internal organs rest, as if the dam were an organic creation, and the scroll case of the turbine a womb or an abdomen wall. As forms of ecoporn, these paintings show the world's body may be exploited just like any other.

The most famous painter of the group was Norman Rockwell, who needed little introduction. He insisted on painting human projects and human bodies, not merely landscapes. Maybe because of his fame, his *Glen Canyon Dam* canvas demands audiences view the dam from an Indian perspective.

The dam is a tourniquet. The fish downstream, the river's lifeblood, will never be able to get by. The dam sprawls like an invader from outer space. Still and all, the painting says the Indians' resolve to survive will serve them in good stead. They confront the massive dam face rather than shrink from it.

Those painters commissioned to beautify Bureau of Reclamation dams were no slouches. Kenneth Callahan, Ralston Crawford, Richard Diebenkorn, Lamar Dodd, and Norman Rockwell received fees for their work that never entered the public record. Their work, by the time it toured the nation as a traveling exhibition, sponsored jointly by the Whitney and the Smithsonian in the early 1970s, already had served its political purpose well enough. The paintings were conceived to be little more than promotional tools—expendable, all but forgotten. They were poorly maintained. Half of the 355 artworks were reported missing in an inventory made in the early 1990s.

Promotional snow jobs occurred at every stage of the frontier process. One wily ad man, Charles Dana Wilber, a Nebraska land speculator, aimed to persuade would-be western immigrants in 1881 that "rain follows the plow." His classic propaganda line is simply a more craven and less-subtle variation of the species of sublimity perpetuated by the nineteenth-century painters and those twentieth-century brushes hired by the Bureau of Reclamation. In every instance, nature needed to be subservient to the national will. A kindly God would be apt to favor the most courageous immigrants with helpful weather.

Often in memory I return to that subliming winter storm, that snowfall in reverse. The warm wind whisked away the snow more swiftly than my next-door neighbor's two-stroke thrower would have done.

If needed, I would volunteer to serve witness to that miraculous event. I would gladly testify. Natural miracles are in short supply these days. In the darkness, though, that wonder visually eluded me.

I wish I had been more intuitive. What I would give now to have crept from bed, switched on the yard lights, and faced the thawing gale.

The American West has been called a resource colony, an arid empire, a raw-materials storehouse for the rest of the world. Former Secretary of the Interior and Arizona Governor Bruce Babbitt said that our western states share "something of third-world economy based on resource extraction."

The federal government, with the tidy paintings it commissioned, aimed to bring about a public-relations makeover. Reacting to the growing power of environmentalism in the 1960s, and the emerging scientific consensus that gave it credence and support, the fed hoped to quell the most strident complaints and keep cheap energy flowing for big business interests. In the inland Northwest where I live and shovel snow, extractive industries have left behind devastated regions and declining communities. The people inhabiting those communities benefited only briefly from corporate largess.

If the craft of public relations has become a runway to consumer trust, then technologies developed during World War II provided the foundation for that runway. Applied sciences, vast engineering feats, and short-run agricultural practices allowed industry to become a domineering force.

The Bureau of Reclamation's aims were imperial. Its grand water projects needed to be dedicated, honored, and rendered iconic by artworks that might grace the nation and be displayed in the halls of federal buildings. The agency's feats prompted celebrations attended by solemnity and pomp.

The Reclamation Art Collection built a none-too-subtle iconography of public lands. Those public lands had to be *reclaimed* to harmonize with Manifest Destiny. To manifest the national destiny to stretch from sea to shining sea, the naive nationalism that fueled expansion in the era had to *take back* from nature—and from the indigenous people—lands that primordial forces long before had claimed.

What preceded that reclamation, that taking back, would have been unacceptable to portray, although Hudson River School painter Thomas Cole showed the way one could try to do so in the sequence he entitled *Progress of Civilization*. In that series, Cole depicted the evolution of humankind in an arc. The arc started from a savage state, then built to scattered communities, to a flourishing civilization, and down at last to a condition of declension or decay, where artifacts and memorials are crumbling and laid waste.

That winter night I witnessed a wind that lifted the snow in my yard and driveway and spirited it away. That winter night I attained a state of awe. The warm wind, blown in from the south, transmogrified the snow and spared me the trouble of shoving and shoveling. It tutored me in the venerable powers of weather to bring about great changes in the land.

To be held up as sublime is to be made to inspire, in the etymological sense of God's respiration, God's breath, a gentle breeze that washes across the worthy recipient. In the sciences, to sublime is to convert a solid to a gas without a liquid phase between. Saints were similarly translated to heaven.

Following the mid-twentieth century, following the slow evaporation of God from the intellectual landscape, some Americans began effectively to worship technology and its products. Still today we see the reverencing of gadgetry. Our highest scientists, engineers, and technicians continue to enjoy relative rank, wealth, and prestige.

The engineering feats that led to Reclamation's dams changed western ecologies and landforms for all time. Reclamation turned to art and artifice to manage its issues, to effect an issues management. Still and all, the Bureau's dam projects — forms of artifice also — hold true beauty for some viewers.

What a high-tech event I beheld aloud that night, even if I missed it with my human eye. I lay in bed and wondered what manner of wind was gathering to blow, what event of weather had struck me silent and still.

In the dark I dozed, planning my assault on the fallen snow with low-tech shovels shaped like plows. Clueless indoors, I listened as the slender miracle occurred. I lay in earshot of water that fell from the sky as a solid and returned to the clouds as gas.

# On Attention

On the shore near Copalis, Washington, we seated ourselves one sunset late in August. Five of us gathered on that Pacific beach to watch the sun slide below the horizon. On the tailgate of Darryl's pickup we found shelter from the wind. It was a crush there. We held our breath and crowded one another. Beneath my shorts I felt the *F* in *Ford*. The springs on the pickup squeaked.

The instant the diminishing sun ball vanished, the green flash glowed and was gone. Not everyone managed to see it. In our party of adults, all hopefully gazing, only three would witness that phenomenon of light. The other two felt pale, shortchanged, frustrated. The final wash of light off the black west fled. It pooled slowly and drained.

Maybe my companions' eyes could not adjust as fast as needed to perceive the gleam that glows when seawater filters the sun's last beam. Maybe they blinked at just the wrong time. Or maybe they were not attending hard enough to earn the renowned green flash. It is elusive and hard to see.

The athlete trains to clear the hurdle. The pianist trembles through her numbers hundreds of times. Painters, sculptors, and smiths devote years to mastering their crafts. Just so, there is an earned aspect to spectacles outdoors. If practice makes perfect, a quality of sharp attention complements the visual privilege. A hunter might put on camouflage and blunder into field or forest, hoping to prove lucky with his gun, but it is rare that he or she does.

For Darryl and me, the quest for the green flash had become a surrogate for the hunt. We had practiced the art of the chase for decades, had pursued warm quarry together since we were eight. We had shot animals and birds, caught fish, picked berries, plucked mushrooms, and found artifacts in old shacks. Instincts toward hunting and gathering surged strong within us.

We were raised in outdoor families. Time spent in the woods or fields, around the campfire at night, were the quality times with our fathers, who modeled enduring behaviors when they told us stories of how they chased, butchered, bagged, or otherwise claimed their deer, elk, and other big quarry. In living rooms and workshops, we gawked at the formerly warm trophies on the walls; we fingered the precious fabric of the stories that lay behind them. We could almost hear the rifles go off, could see and smell the powder burn.

From those fathers, and for their sake, we had learned to pay attention, keep our counsel to ourselves, stay quiet and wait for just the right shot. Our inner jabbering needed to be silenced whenever we hoped to grow attentive in the woods. At home, too, when the television was blaring or the supper dishes a-clatter, we'd had to learn to attend. We had to wait for the grace note, the muted statement of encouragement or praise. We knew it would never do to snap off rounds in haste; words were as precious as powder and lead.

Our fathers taught us to keep our mouths shut and listen because we had so much to learn, and they knew that learning the habit well requires attention. I set my sights on stilling the inner voice in meditative moments, whether swimming, hiking, stalking, working, or simply breathing. Exercising hard today still takes me to a place of focus, a zone that narrows the field of vision, that builds a psychology of attentiveness similar to the hunt, akin to the feeling of vigilance that goes with the fight-or-flight response to danger. Moving into a state of right concentration requires a planned and practiced manner.

Attention and patience as social attributes seem to be on the wane. And some of us are concerned. I've known grown men to grimace and pound desks because the chips in their computers just don't go fast enough to meet their expectations, to fulfill their heightened needs. Nor am I much better. To cop an obsolete locution, I have "looked my eyes out" when a friend pointed to a whitetail buck's ear twitching in a field. The animal rested in the shade, my friend said, its antlers like branches on a low tree. I looked and looked but could not distinguish those bony protrusions from surrounding bushes and the twigs. I tried to take in the entire landscape, but that detail escaped me.

Healthy adults, more than a dozen of them, all walking toward the same aspen grove, failed to see the sharp-shinned hawk blaze from the sky, slam the cedar waxwing, and follow it to the sod. They missed the waxwing's ruptured feathers rocking earthward, did not witness the hawk lift its prey to the limb of a quaking aspen and set to work to pluck the waxwing's breast.

The word *attention* itself shows us what we lack. Mindfulness, a noun that's rare to most of us except for Buddhists, comes up in my word-hoard. It means to ponder, to apply patience, to grow watchful in the here-and-now. Its root word, the French verb *attendre*, means to wait. Maybe the deferring of our gratification is what grows harder every day, following the onslaught of commercials urging us to satisfy our craving in an instant. Give in; just do it.

Holy leaders have gathered students around themselves and spoken, but not all of the students could understand the messages being conveyed. We have the words of the Buddha to consult, but we often fail to perceive the message. Mindfulness and concentration as ways of living require a discipline that escapes us all too often. Youth can get in the way sometimes.

Children, allegedly in record numbers, are suffering Attention Deficit Disorder, a condition that pediatricians are linking with hyperactivity. While it may be true that "schizophrenia never takes a holiday," drug companies are making enormous profits from physicians' diagnoses. As technology enhances our response times, we humans desire to run at faster rates just to keep up.

Maybe the resulting hyperactivity is causing young people's attentions to feel overspent. Anxious and unfocused humans can't stand to wait—whether to get our way, have our say, become adults, or to claim our due. We gauge attention, like the reach of a suspension bridge, by its proverbial span. Some of us children might never grow up. Big boys on bicycles who hunt for distance, who gather miles as if they were tangible trophies to be borne aloft for neighbors and friends, rarely take the time to truly witness what they pass.

Teachers in urban schoolyards in France, driven to distraction by their frenzied students, admonish them with the double *Attendez, attendez!* The phrase has more a sense of *Be patient* than literally *Wait, wait.* The teachers are not urging their shrill charges to remain, so much as to slow down, cool it. They are asking rowdy kids to focus and find what the moment might make known.

With little authority I make these observations, for I have been a poor fisherman, one who finally gave it up as a sport that wholly bored me. I had too little focus to sustain that particular chase. I felt I needed other game.

It was the same with spectator sports. I enjoy playing ball games, but am unable to comprehend how watchers can get keyed up enough to leap from their seats and roar at a screen when a specific play is made. Even today in middle age, it startles me to be party to such behavior. I grow embarrassed to be human. My friend Hart Rink, a German émigré, with no scent of rancor, just a wry wink, calls sports broadcast on television "the national stupor." Neither Hart nor I have learned that particular art of attention.

In retrospect, I might have been focusing on myself while I was trying to catch fish. Of course, I was the wrong focus of attention. Fishing works to reconnect us to the food we eat; it requires a right mindfulness; it calls for a way of living that is not distracted in its accountability. To play a game is to live; to watch a game is to live vicariously. The first pursuit may allow for liberation; the second can be a trap, when blighted by commercial appeals.

Attention is involved in all we know, and what we know is chiefly what we see. But there's seeing and then there's seeing wholly, viewing truly, transcending the vale of tears the old saints named. I will take my knowledge seasoned fully with the senses. The inner eye is a mere construct, for my meager money, a metaphor for spiritual harlequins. I, the empirical I, need to have firsthand observation of the nonphenomenal world to tender it its due.

Water is a fine place to focus the attention. Its textures and colors are subtle, its sounds and smells more delicate than the jarring confrontations of television, lurid films, and video games. To take chances, to accept spray in the face as a way to become less wet behind the ears, is now a theory underlying Outward Bound and other hoods-in-the-woods programs. Even corporate trainers are drenching novices these days. Water is the telltale element in all of our relations with visible nature, as Ishmael in *Moby-Dick* knows so well.

Those who value the green flash are prepared to wait in the wind

and spray. They are content to take a seat and risk distraction by raucous flocks of plovers and gulls. Just attend. On that August evening
when we were studying the horizon, stunt kites were diving. Birds
were swirling by the thousands, chasing sand fleas on the shore or
schools of herring in the shoals. We had to background the gulls,
plovers and kites, tune them out as bad distractions. As Robert Mac-
Farlane has noted of previous generations, "attention was a form of
devotion and noticing continuous with worship." Maybe on the Pacific rim that day we were worshiping the sun, its life-giving force,
and never knew it.

Imagine keeping the green flash in view every hour of your life.
As the Earth turned, you might hover in one place and see the globe
rolling beneath you. You could line up sun and Earth like rifle-sights,
orbit the solar system's sun alongside our home planet as it spun. This
world's oceans, covering two-thirds of its surface, would be massive
lenses to color all you see. Is there a deeper green to the Indian Ocean
than to the Mediterranean? Ice, too, at the poles, would be bound to
filter light and transmit a new shade, however faint.

Annie Dillard wrote, as if scales had fallen from her eyes, about
learning at last to see muskrats. She stalked with patience and craft,
studied their habits and haunts, but finally just discovered how to ease
into muskrat ways and space. Out in the wild, birds and animals tend
to seize on motion more readily than color. Whether the prey is sen-
tient or numb, one needs to hold still when stalking, become a statue
and freeze, before the perceiver becomes the perceived. Not that I
have learned to put any of these lessons into accurate practice. From
Dillard I learned to get in the way of grace, to stalk opportunities, become an outdoor opportunivore. Last year I began to see river otters
in my bioregion everywhere. Or maybe I just began to tune in to otters all around me. Maybe at last I learned how to out-attend them.

First I saw a family of otters swimming in a channel of the Koo-
tenai River outside Bonner's Ferry, Idaho. In that wildlife refuge, human visitors must have weaned them of some of their native caution.
I crouched on a ridge above the water where they romped. I kept still,
tried to become invisible. They chattered and thumped while clam-
bering to shore.

Weeks later, a pair of adult otters materialized from liquid swirls while I was kayaking to stare me down at Bonnie Lake in the channeled scablands near where I live. They swam close, territorial, looked me in the eye and nudged me from my comfort zone. I pulled paddle from water and held it out before me, just to be safe and sure. I had heard that summer about a young man inner tubing the Green River, near Auburn on the coast, who got bitten dozens of times when he floated through a family of otters. That story reminded me that otters are close relatives of wolverines, weasels, minks, and skunks.

Still later that spring in my kayak I paced an otter — did my best not to chase it — for hundreds of yards down the Palouse River near the ghost town of Elberton. Near my paddle it surfaced, confronted me, dove one time, then paced me as the current bore us toward the Columbia River and the Pacific. A kind of watery vertigo ensued. Either it was relishing my company or luring me from its family and home. That whiskery creature disappeared at last.

After years of finding only droppings colored red by crawfish shells, I was coming up with river otters every flooding place I gazed. It could have been coincidence. Maybe that year was a good year for otter litters in my land. Maybe I just needed to wait for scales to drop from my judging eyes.

Darryl filled up plastic glasses with wine on the beach. We were having a tailgate party, between Ocean City and Copalis, after the big event. We were celebrating success in our endeavor to pursue and capture the last sunrays. Sand grains were growing airborne, landing in our cups with splashes out of earshot. We lipped sand as we drank, gritted it between our teeth. We had waited entire lifetimes for this chance.

"Welcome to the Green Flash Club." Darryl shook hands all around in a pretense of solemnity. His somberness stood out as a pretense because there is no club, his gravity a charade because the moment was not solemn but joyous — a species of joy that would bear no scrutiny or breakdown. We had attended closely to the horizon. We had let every distraction slip away, held our breaths, and it paid off. The wind and surf applauded. Sand grains sang.

The green flash, to my eyes, is really neither flashy nor is it green. A hushed color, it is not as loud as money. Even as a kind of cultural currency, it may never be redeemed. It confers no tangible wisdom, nor is it an emblem of religious conversion or a manifestation of the divine, animated or otherwise.

It is a swift glint as the sun's face sinks, a revelation that betrays the expanse of this planet's watery body, a hint of aquamarine given then gone, a sudden leap of revelation that the world is vastly larger than it seems.

# Under the Sign of Aries

Orting, Washington, is rehearsing for calamity. People in this town northwest of Mount Rainier will have an estimated thirty minutes to vacate if the mountain melts its glaciers to a slurry or blows its snowy dome. The second tallest in the forty-eight states, and the highest of the glaciated peaks, Rainier worries scientists. It shoulders more ice and snow than all the other Cascade crags combined. The town lies smack in the path of a likely lahar, a big flood of heavy mud that volcanoes typically trigger. Worse yet, bridges over the Carbon and Puyallup rivers congest the only car routes out of Orting. The more diligent citizens are trying to organize dry runs, mass departures in the event of a cataclysm, succeeding in lowering their flight times from forty-three minutes to thirty-seven. Meanwhile, in evident defiance of nature, more and more urban exiles are moving into Orting every year, an ongoing influx of people that exasperates blacksmith Darryl Nelson, from whose bearded face wry ridicule for the county planners erupts. "They ought to send the flatlanders back home." Hefting a pair of tongs in an asbestos glove, he waves the sooty tool toward Orting. "And then they ought to order the rest to stay the hell away." A former flatlander himself, Darryl is a refugee from the crush of population in Seattle. From his forge he draws a clot of hot iron, slaps it on an anvil, begins to strike. The clamor of his hammering fills the shop. He's an imposing gnome of a man—ruddy, bald, and mostly jolly—girded today in safety glasses and steel-toed work boots of the sort that motorcyclists wear.

Sparks thrown by the blower fly from his forge, which resembles a small volcano. His t-shirt, featuring an anvil and the slogan *Semper Dur*, sports burn holes from airborne embers, a constant hazard in his line of work. I insert my earplugs, step way back, and give him room to let the sparks fly.

As a child Darryl cut his teeth as an artist-to-be by gazing at nature and learning its varied shapes by heart. We became friends when we were eight. In North Dakota where he was born, in the wilds of eastern Washington and the high Cascades, also on the tide flats of Puget Sound, he discovered an interspecies society of sorts. One of his earliest jobs was training hunting dogs. In our Seattle high school he crafted jewelry from copper, silver, and brass. In lieu of college he trained as a farrier and learned to shoe horses. In later years he fused his several pursuits by whaling on hot iron with ever-greater grace. Mammals, birds, and leaves emerged, gardens and bestiaries whole. As a journeyman blacksmith, he pooled his money with others to fly in master smiths who would pilot hands-on workshops. Only later did he give up on the horseshoeing, move to the country, and begin to peddle his rustic hand-wrought products at county fairs and a co-op store he founded in Seattle.

His earliest labors bore trivets, bottle openers, dinner bells, and snakes. One of those first pieces in my office holds an edge. It's a skinning knife, sinister in its curve and made from one-inch industrial cable whose braid, evident in the supple handle, tapers to a sharp tip at the business end.

During that early phase, Darryl felt compelled to accept most custom jobs that came his way. If musicians detest playing weddings and parties, smiths feel the same about making window grates. Today he enjoys enough custom work to ratchet back on everyday production and on hired help.

He pauses to scowl at the object in his tongs. It has cooled from orange to black, it has shed its scale or flake, and it is taking shape in ways few others can see. Now his rod of iron needs another heat, and so he shoves it back in the forge, under a pile of thermal stones where the blower throws its glow.

He wheezes a little, removes his gloves and glasses, and folds his hands over his belly. He inclines his head, squints his eyes, and twists his mouth. He rarely gestures when he speaks, a useless urban affectation. Every declaration prompts a smile. The smile is the idle he returns to, the neutral between gears.

City folks, he says, are filling Orting faster than they can ever evacuate. Highway bottlenecks will never draw off vehicles fast enough. Refugees from Seattle and Tacoma, streams of commuters and retirees craving their pieces of paradise, end up trashing the stuff they love. We could inoculate against them. Other medical analogies come to mind. The flatlanders are like microbes, their sprawl and strip malls a species of disease. In the coastal corridors they favor, earthquakes throng along a fault line, tsunamis threaten from the sea, the Cascades grumble. Beneath Orting rests an ancient forest, trees entombed by lahars far back in geologic time, discovered by some drudges excavating a foundation for a building. People say the trees are standing *upright*. And Rainier certainly will explode again, as it did a brief century and a half ago. The Cascades are far from dormant, Mount St. Helens proved in 1980, even though people like to comfort themselves by believing that they are, even after that eruption killed fifty-seven humans and thousands of deer, elk, bears, and smaller mammals and birds, all of whose populations have rebounded.

From a distance of two hundred miles, Darryl and I witnessed that upheaval. We were trout fishing with Harold and others on May eighteenth in north-central Washington. We mistook the boom for a blast from a mineshaft. Only a couple hours later did a transistor radio give us the news. We packed up fast and headed south, hooking across the Cascades toward Seattle just in time. Driving with our families and friends, we dodged to the west, in advance of the mile-high wall of ash, the darkness at noon that blew so far upcountry.

Darryl and his wife had already severed their suburban Seattle roots and moved to find their little piece of paradise, where they raised turkeys and horses, roses and golden retrievers, escaping the hurry-up-and-wait routine of Interstate 5, the slow-and-go traffic, the Seattle buzz. Now the buzz is taking a run at them and their ranch, beneath the western shadow of Mount Rainier.

Darryl and Suzan live in a house surrounded by Douglas-firs, vine maple, blackberry canes, and alders. Empty-nesters, they raised two kids and now help to rear their grandchildren nearby. Where elk used to bugle and cougars prowl, where an occasional black bear snuck a snack, country squires now build McMansions and topple trees to improve their views of Mount Rainier.

In a raw patch across the highway, a machine called a feller-buncher is working. It grasps a cottonwood, sheers it at ground level, flops it horizontal to the landscape, and strips off every branch. The feller-buncher looks like a robot, its operator concealed by struts within the belly of the machine.

Back behind the Nelson spread, a group of meth cooks has fled after five years, not ousted for endangering neighbors, but for failing to pay the piper of rising property taxes. The land lies quieter since those wakeful citizens stopped shooting guns off after dark. Still, the hissing of jake-brakes, the droning of planes out of McChord Air Force Base, blend and blur with the daily work.

One loud chore segues to the next. Horse to forge, tractor to anvil, hay bales to the crashing trip hammer—that massive hydraulic maul that shapes hot metal with speedy repeated blows. From his converted garage, Darryl runs one business, Meridian Forge Blacksmithing School, where students enroll for three-day courses. Sometimes he puts his students up in a bunkhouse, a frame shack the Eatonville Logging Company hauled by flatcar into various logging sites. The bunkhouse recalls the California drifters John Steinbeck drew—the wood stove, the card games and the smelly dog, the glove of Vaseline to keep a hand soft for the wife back home. Darryl's funky bunkhouse now is busy with bison knickknacks and kitsch ads he has collected over the decades.

Outside the door of both houses, alpenglow tints Mount Rainier in hues of magenta and peach. The mountain overtops the house and grounds, lending its image to the blacksmith business, Fire Mountain Forge. On this spread outside Eatonville, Darryl and Suzan have lived and worked for thirty years, running beef cattle and saddle horses, trying to keep dogs off the road.

Darryl has a regional name and a growing national status for his custom ornamental forging. Lodges, stores, cities, museums, and wealthier homeowners in Portland and Seattle hire him to build fences, ornaments, andirons, and doors. In London, the gate of the Globe Theatre sports one of his pieces, as does the National Underground Railroad Freedom Center in Cincinnati, a museum of more than one hundred thousand square feet. Best known for his heavy installation work and animal heads, he has gotten wide exposure from renovations at Timberline Lodge on Mount Hood in Oregon.

As a rationalist he disputes the efficacy of muses, inspirations, and visitations from the divine. "Move the metal till the metal moves you," some fellow blacksmiths advise their protégés. "That's bullshit," he grins, "but it's a great corny thing to say to those who want to find a spiritual dimension in the work." Such woo-woo nonsense too easily dupes the mutable masses, he suggests.

Glass artisan Dale Chihuly, whose Pilchuck Glass School north of Seattle enjoys great institutional favor, "has snowed the public into thinking of his work as religious. He got in an accident, lost an eye, opened several schools, and now puts his name on the products his students produce."

Darryl is both more modest and more proud than that. Then, too, the public has been slower to accept his chosen medium as a form of art. Iron is black. It does not filter light. It can't be fashioned to please those whose chief need is to match the carpets and drapes. "Custom work satisfies the artist and craftsman," he confesses, "while production work satisfies the monetary needs of a business." Some rural-nesters have modest monetary needs. A jug of wine, a loaf of bread, a jumble of machinery and trees, a mountain view.

Hired to travel out of state to demonstrate his craft, Darryl most often teaches how to shape the heads of rams, bears, coyotes, and other species of charismatic megafauna. Guiding students to simulate a grizzly bear can be frustrating if they have never seen one. In California he proposed that his students simply heat a square of iron stock and "push away everything that doesn't look like a bear." How easily he could say so. To describe the process that way presupposes the students have observed bears and remembered their heads. Grizzlies have dish faces; black bears have longer snouts like dogs.

Darryl has seen both species close at hand—first as a big-game hunter, later as a near neighbor of Northwest Trek Wildlife Park, where predators pace cages for several hundred thousand people every year. The Trek claims to own all the indigenous species that ever inhabited the Pacific Northwest. Visitors may ride a tram through forests and meadows to witness big, hoofed critters. During a visit we made one spring, a grizzly bear, a young sow, took a sapling like a drumstick in her jaws and tapped it up and down on an outdoor log in a spacey, almost autistic way that seemed to delight the lookers-on. During another visit the outside wolverine cage was being cleaned, and the wolverines shunted into a kind of terrarium that the keepers wheeled indoors. Just before closing time we crept into that neon-lit space. The wolverines snarled and charged us, their heartfelt hatred hybridized by fear and rage.

"Study nature," Darryl says, when one of his students asks how to draw out the animals from the iron. "You won't find many smiths living in Manhattan who can do bears or rams or trilliums."

Such creatures perish on the burgeoning I-5 corridor. Here today, gone tomorrow, indigenous species are being shoved aside, made to surrender to invasive weeds like Armenian blackberries and Scotch broom, exotic birds like starlings and house sparrows, predatory mammals like opossums that ravage ground-nesting fowl. For every native creature edged out by an opportunistic invader like these, loss of habitat will take five or ten. If suburban sprawl gives Darryl fits, it makes native animals die outright. We humans intuit extinction crises; we suffer from them in ways we find it difficult to fathom. Animals ourselves, we might eat ourselves from the inside out at times, gnawing our own stomachs raw, much as foxes chew off their own legs to escape a trap.

Art tries to offer compensations, consolations. If words are weightless, dances vanish as soon as they're performed, and paintings dry and crack and burn, iron is a more permanent artistic sign. Drawn bright from the fire of Earth itself, weighty iron endures—which might explain why arty and ornamental forging is held in low esteem among dilettantes and aficionados.

Iron lasts. It has durability. It also is functional, though functionality can be an artistic kiss of death. Darryl claims that the U.S. government, which funds artists through the National Endowment for the Arts (NEA), defines art as that which has no function. Until recently, he was right, embittered from feeding long on a thwarted outlook that goes back decades. The NEA now has a unit that funds Traditional and Folk Art. Darryl's art has a function of its own. When it mimics nature, his art is making up for species or habitats going or gone. If bears no longer prowl around and scare us, he may replicate them in iron, draw them from the fire.

People who have never labored for a living often hold the nasty notion that those who work with their hands must be callous and coarse, that all they know of taste must lie in their mouths, and that even the craftiest smiths and artisans must be hobbling clods like old

Hephaistos, deity of the forge. Such stereotyping does not apply to Darryl Nelson, in whom ready wit and common sense compete for equal time. Much as he likes to pay homage to the rational, he has a nostalgic streak that indulges in pagan particulars. Like crippled Hephaistos, too, he lists a little when he walks. No doubt it would flatter him to be compared to that forceful god of volcanoes, that keeper of Earth's fire. The old Greek god forged the armor for Achilles, the trident for Poseidon, a breastplate for Hercules, and a scepter for his father Zeus. Frustrated, rebuffed in his seduction of the goddess Athena, he spilled his hapless seed upon the dirt.

A mere eight generations ago, Darryl's patron crag erupted—according to the traveler Theodore Winthrop who came through the territory in 1853—scattering ash and fertilizing all of eastern Washington. It blew its top. New life sprang from it, as farmers found after Mount St. Helens blew. The cinders, fine as talcum, hold nutrients essential for building soil and growing plants. It has blown its snowy dome for many audiences throughout geological time.

Darryl chooses to live beneath the Mount Rainier volcano, he named his business after it, and he runs a forge whose eruptions mimic the fiery mountain's moods. Geography has molded his character. Images of forges hearken back to domestic gods of hearth and home, to a work ethic with roots in Protestant practice, and to the polar wellsprings of creativity and ruin.

Alice James, one of Darryl's female students, said, "His forge was never off. Even if he wasn't doing anything that required the forge, it was there to remind him that's what you do. The roar of the fire kept you focused." He was born under the sign of Aries, he reminds me, whose symbol is the full-curl ram. And those folks ruled by Aries often end up being subjects of the planet Mars, the war planet, whose envoys can flame out and scorch fast.

At last I manage to distract him from the herd of concerns goaded by the invasive flatlanders, by the town of Orting and its reckless inhabitants. I want him to talk to me about Timberline Lodge and Silcox Hut on Mount Hood, where he has done so much work. He sets down his emerging ram's head for the day, and we move to the house.

He is a coffee man. He operates his own espresso maker with pride and care, and can cope with caffeine late in the day. Deferring to me, though, he has blended a batch of rum batter to take the edge off a winter evening spent standing in his drafty shop. He washes his hands with Lava soap and drifts to the kitchen. In a marble-bottomed bowl, a betta fish stirs, fanning a tangle of waterweeds. A German shepherd barks for supper outside.

Samples of Darryl's ironwork make his home a one-man show. Wall sconces and magazine racks invite human touch, and massive planter racks, identical to those he crafted for the Seattle sidewalk in front of the original Nordstrom's store, dominate one corner. Hand-wrought knives and forks in the kitchen drawers darken the silver table service, and decorative frames on the walls display Danish plates. A dragon's face on a bottle opener appears to breathe out fire. A stout lamp, all iron grape leaves and shadowy filigrees, supports a thong-laced parchment shade.

The feel is rustic, the décor all Western, a Rorschach test that puts viewers in certain moods. In conversation that night, I dare to question the value of bull riding for building skills on a working ranch, and Darryl rears up to defend rodeo against citified detractors like me. Many years have passed since he and I chased birds and girls together, so much fond water gone.

A year later we meet with our wives for a weekend on Mount Hood, unpack our bags in rooms at the six-thousand-foot-high Timberline Lodge, where he has credit in exchange for his ironwork. We find no jet skis, ATVs, or traffic jams. No frantic commuters or rehearsals for calamity. The drapes, the bedspreads, and rugs retain the original Timberline flower motifs — spruce, trillium, monkshood, gentian, Solomon seal, pine needles, and pinecones.

Late in March, the weather is favoring us. We move to the hot tub outdoors and gaze at the mountain. Its west face is flushed with a deep Pacific sunset, the alpenglow so striking it almost seems to transmit sound. Snow is eight feet deep on the alpine flats, higher yet where it slid from the steep roof.

Built in 1936 and 1937, Timberline stands as the supreme example of art distilled from nature. "Bear heads, ram heads, emerge from the design work of the lodge as the snow melts — simulating nature's emergence from winter," Darryl points out, clutching a mug of coffee even as he soaks.

The lodge is a product of the Works Progress Administration (WPA) of Franklin Roosevelt, a New Deal work-relief project for the indigent. Four hundred men and women, staying in two-week rotations that allowed everyone to share the wealth, labored for ninety cents an hour, besides their rooms and board. They slept twelve miles down the mountain in tents, rode to the lodge upright in flatbed trucks, clutching to the rails and one another.

The base camp where the workers stayed, like Steinbeck's camp in *The Grapes of Wrath*, made a town called Government Camp. A village by that name survives. In 1936 it held walled and floored tents, a kitchen, a mess hall, a quartermaster's store, showers with hot and cold water, and an infirmary with a male nurse in charge. "The artisans themselves, Americans out of work, many came from the shipyards and the railroads," Darryl says.

As the lodge's third-generation blacksmith, he speaks with all the conviction of one participating in a great succession. "They were asked to create decorative elements for the first time ever." The result was a noble proletarian art, the modest products of lumpen labor, handicrafts that more than hold up today. To observe the lodge's opening in September 1937, an event attended by President Franklin Roosevelt and Eleanor Roosevelt, the Federal Theatre performed original dances.

The Forest Service oversees Timberline Lodge, whose features bear comparison to the national forests. The Friends of Timberline formed from admirers in 1975 to catalogue the extant crafts and art objects, and to oversee the restoration of those that had been damaged or lost. One hundred and eighty-one pieces of ironwork remain, which is where Darryl comes in.

Some of the Friends had seen his work in Portland and Cannon Beach and extolled him to the Forest Service. The agency has been a prickly partner at times. Installing handrails, in the entryway of the upslope warming hut named Silcox Hut, Darryl bolted the rail to a rock wall and was scolded, his architect almost fired. How else install a rail? Had he not used a handrail, he would have violated the Americans with Disabilities Act of 1990. He growls and woofs when he speaks about regulatory overkill and bureaucratic red tape.

Americans have gotten wind of the ways the Forest Service squanders federal forests, builds miles and miles of roads that fracture wildlife habitat, and sells trees to bidders far below market rates. The agency has subsidized the timber industry and the building trades. Senator Frank Church wrote, "Past experience indicates that the Forest Service performs best when they are being watched closely by those people with an interest in their programs." Darryl and the Friends of Timberline have interests and are watching closely.

Both Silcox Hut and Timberline Lodge embody an aesthetic that is coming to be known as Cascadian. The American Institute of Architects defines it as "native rock work, large timber and steeply pitched roofs in a rustic manner." Civil engineers define it, more generally, as "a style deriving from European chateaux and alpine architecture." Neither definition satisfies.

To define Cascadian arts, one has to factor in the decorative elements. Darryl has opinions aplenty. "What the workers were producing might not be regarded as art, but they should be considered artisans, not craftsmen. I like to say it takes skill to do a craft, which is not necessarily true for artists."

This personal rift between art and craft — between the functional and decorative, the practical and the finesse of haute couture — is constantly shooting off sparks in his conversations about aesthetics. If he were a man who liked to dip snuff, he would be spitting tobacco juice to punctuate his opinions. Instead he sighs. "Other artists do bears, but they don't put in the details. They make abstract bears."

All four of us lean back in the hot tub, a little dizzy from the heat, working to discern shapes emerging from the steam around us. A bull's head on the building materializes, much like grotesque waterspouts formed from gargoyles on European cathedrals. The bull gazes at us in the tub below.

The shingle style of American architecture became known as the *rustic picturesque*, a relatively unsophisticated method that was proposed for this lodge originally. Factions in the federal government battled over what sort of art and artists most earned and deserved to benefit from public funds. The Forest Service surprised its pundits and its federal overseers alike by bringing in a team of architects. They adopted a style named the *stately picturesque*.

These architectural terms remind me of Karen. She turns a stately stare my way and shoots a beam from the fog of sleep. More than six feet tall, much of that height taken up by leg, she is something to behold. But we are dragging after a five-hour drive and a soak in the hot tub, our necks rubbery.

Darryl grins, smacks lips, savors his latte, and regards the stars. The finish work that embellishes the lodge, he goes on, is a hodgepodge of Indian and Oregon pioneer heritage. We are soaking in this hot tub near the end of the Oregon Trail, I remember just then. Karen is wearing a one-piece suit, floral print, modesty having determined that the bikini stay at home.

We rise from the hot tub and towel off. The water has made everyone groggy, but Darryl is going full-bore, ordering more coffee, cueing us. He is in his element here at Timberline—letting go the vagaries of bad planning and growth management around his home in western Washington, shutting out the sounds of passing trucks and Air Force jets, leaving the ranching chores to others for the moment.

The lodge is a sanctuary that invites all comers to enter a still point where art meets craft. Hands-on contact is not only permitted; it is expected and encouraged, amid the wood and iron, the textiles and tile, the glasswork and stone. No uniformed curators come round to hush and censor, no security guards to make us stand far off. Time stops, as John Keats saw it on his famous Grecian urn, affording visitors respite from their transience and toil.

We heave our bodies up a flight of stairs, past stout cedar newel-posts crowned with carvings of eagles, beavers, owls, grouse, and deer fawns—each animal holding its place in a web of ecological relations, each one marked as predator or prey. The banisters and support beams bear the marks from broadax and foot adze where workmen shaved them, beginning in June of 1936. Visitors' hands have burnished the native fir, pine, hemlock, cedar, and white oak to a high gloss.

We are still stirring. In this National Historic Landmark, we head toward the Blue Ox Bar for a nightcap.

Paul Bunyan, the legendary Midwest woodcutter, lent his mascot Babe the Ox to the bar. The weighty wooden chairs with leather seats take two hands to slide from beneath the table. Bunyan and his ox materialize in a seven-by-twelve-foot opus sectile, a style of painted and fused glasswork.

In the 1940s the bar was a bottle club, before the state of Oregon legalized liquor by the drink. The logging motif reminds me of the novel *Sometimes a Great Notion*, the saga of the Stamper family bent on cutting every tree. Hank Stamper the elder, in the novel by Oregon native Ken Kesey, erects a sign outside his riverside home that reads, "Never give a inch." In a tiny irony, the timber culture is yielding to environmental ethics.

At all the state's universities, the University of Oregon in particular, students are learning what sustainability means. It means to perpetuate the ecological and cultural values cherished by the region and the state, following more rash ancestors who perfected a practice of cut-and-run logging on public lands. Boomtowns turned to busts in that cycle; moist pockets of evergreens grew drier and briar-grown. The University of Oregon hosts an annual environmental law conference, known among green cognoscenti as E-Law.

At that university too, the first-generation Timberline blacksmith, Orion B. Dawson, built the magnificent Hall Memorial gates with their pinecone motifs for the entrance to the Knight Library. Dawson gave up an opera career for the Federal Art Project of the WPA. Once the construction of Timberline Lodge was complete, he pled with docents and federal overseers that the older smiths in his Portland workshop continue to have gainful work.

Besides Timberline, the regional lodges that best showcase Cascadian art include Crater Lake, Paradise on Mount Rainier, and Lake Quinault in the Olympics. But harmonious conceptual continuity between them "was not premeditated," Darryl claims. It was as if their origins had an organic basis, or were geographically determined. It is as if all of them were products of place.

"Once they were built, the American Institute of Architects looked at their expression as unique, retrospective, more than the sum of their parts." Those parts include rams' heads that adorn brackets on the door of a bread-warming oven built in the Timberline fireplace. Darryl replicated the original brackets, which had gotten badly sprung from hard use across the decades.

"When I duplicate something being replaced in the lodge, I have to put some kind of identifying mark or date so they can tell fifty years from now what's a replica and what's original" — his work resembles the products of the WPA that much. "I make fire tools for this purpose, duplicating them for rooms with fireplaces, using a Timberline ram head motif."

Those ram heads look familiar to me. The slender necks, horns lowered like battering rams, the body language signaling neither pure aggression nor simple self-defense. The ram is the symbol of Aries, I remember, a fire sign in the astrological chart. There is no better totem to be had for Darryl, who often seems so eager to butt heads. Rams, unlike sheep, share with goats a randy manner, a feral toughness. Metal's resistance to breaking under repeated bending and twisting forces is measured in kilojoules. The ram is *semper dur.*

When I ask Darryl to characterize the Cascadian ironwork, he replies it is "medieval craftsman style." I know what a craftsman house style is, with its low rafters and heavy beams, its dark and brooding aspect, so I have a start. "Cascadian," he elaborates, "adds to the craftsman style a rougher finish and line that is less clean."

Then I begin to see. Adze marks add character to planks and beams — and chamfering adds strokes to the newel-posts that otherwise might have been sanded clean — just as rustic design work on the iron adds its own rustic touch. It becomes a proletarian signature, a deliberate smudge, an integral part of the art. If form follows function in design work, then function dictates form outright in the architecture and art that is coming to be known as the Cascadian.

"Boy, they sure don't make stuff like this anymore," one of Timberline's visitors said, even while Darryl and another smith were bending over a replica railing and installing it. Russell Maugans, Darryl's mentor and the second-generation Timberline blacksmith, treasured the naïve comment.

He turned to Darryl. "That man just paid us the highest compliment that could be paid. I didn't want to contradict him." Maugans — a World War II bomber pilot first, a commercial pilot second, and a blacksmith third — grew so engaged in Timberline's restoration that he came out of retirement and relit his forge, but he died before the work could be finished.

As the third-generation Timberline blacksmith, Darryl wears his soot honestly. The initial builders of the lodge, many of them, came from industrial backgrounds, just as he spent an interminable seven months with the Boeing Company, that Seattle-based maker of military and commercial jets. Many men of the Vietnam generation, especially those who did not go to college after graduating from Seattle-area high schools, worked for "the Lazy B." Like his father and brother before him—both of them now dead—Darryl tried his hand at Boeing, but unlike them he felt caged.

Still, he is a workingman. His fingers and hands suffer from heavy hammering's impact on the sacs that hold the lubricating sinovial fluid for the joints. A childhood victim of asthma, he self-medicates in imaginative ways for the illness, and every day he inhales a heady share of particulates that flow from his anvil and forge. Had he stayed on with Boeing, Darryl would be counting down the days until retirement. Middle-aged and older men lag behind in factories, which rarely reward skills earned through practicing and mastering crafts. Indeed, they offer disincentives to skills.

Instead, Darryl discovered in himself an artistic bent. Like his precursors during the Great Depression, he has given his best to public institutions that many people visit, realizing he is a part of a legacy much larger than himself, and that his work needs to be made publicly accessible. "My interest since I was a small child has always been animals and nature, and I have learned there is no end to what you can do with hot metal." After tracking his replications of nature for several decades, I agree that ironwork is one of the most neglected arts. "Other artisans cop attitudes because my work is figurative or representational, and some want to do only contemporary, conceptual art that you have to squint to see. They are abstract snobs."

# The Silver Valley

"The worst are the racing thoughts." That's how Cass Davis describes his health problems since he was "leaded" in the early 1970s by smelter fallout from northern Idaho's Bunker Hill silver mine.

I am visiting his family home in Pinehurst, Idaho, where the EPA is replacing the contaminated lawn in his mother's yard. First the agency workers scrape the landscape bare and then they truck in loads of clean fill.

Cass spent time in nearby Smelterville as well, but it was in Pinehurst when he was nine that the heaviest fallout hit. Silver Valley children, tests by the Centers for Disease Control confirmed, had the highest blood-lead levels ever recorded in humans. Many of them and their children still live in houses whose heating ducts, crawl spaces, and carpeting test high in lead.

"Racing thoughts is the way I talk about the ADHD," explains Cass. We look down at our shoes and the dirt in the yard. He and I were close friends before I moved away from the town of Moscow, Idaho. Cass and I plucked morel mushrooms, danced with abandon in granges and parks, hiked and argued and wrestled until we gasped. We gathered signatures and picketed City Hall. He trusted me enough to meet his family and take me to their homes.

Attention-deficit hyperactivity disorder (ADHD), among a range of other woes, makes it tough for Cass to focus—on words, on work, even on sex. His thoughts race. "Before I know it, the erection has fallen," Cass confesses gently, with neither pity nor bravado. For a reflective moment he is still. Then the words rush again, his thoughts race, and we're off to tour the Silver Valley.

East of Spokane on Interstate 90, in Shoshone County, Idaho, the south fork of the Coeur d'Alene River threads its way through the

Silver Valley, at one time the most productive silver mining site on Earth. For a full century, mining corporations reaped sweet profits amid backwoods burgs that are struggling to stay alive today. Many of the fortunes and grandest homes in Spokane are the products of Idaho's nineteenth-century mines.

In the Silver Valley you can see the mining industry's footprint in the twenty-one-mile Superfund site, the second largest site in the nation. You can find it in the sterile waters, the damaged people, the dead swans, and you can find it on the beaches of the Spokane River more than fifty miles away. You can hear it in the voice of Cass's mother, Corinne Davis, who remembers when she went "to track meets at the school and wasn't able to see across the track field." Some events, she said, got canceled due to heavy smelter smoke. She learned to cope. "You would hope for a good windstorm before the track meet."

Whether companies or governments should be liable for the cleanup, following more than a century of pollution, is a question several high-stakes trials have attempted to answer. Estimates of the clean-up costs range from fifty million to three billion dollars. The interested parties in the trial—the tribes, the mining companies, the State of Idaho, and the federal government—became expert at maligning each other, politely of course, and the EPA took plenty of hits from all sides for its management of the complicated clean-up tasks.

Residents of Spokane are learning, meanwhile, that the beaches of the upper Spokane River contain the highest concentrations of poisonous metals on any waterway in the state. Washington Governor Chris Gregoire's office demanded from the federal government and the State of Idaho that the Spokane River be considered in any remediation plans. Residents of Spokane and Coeur d'Alene also are learning that the bottom of Lake Coeur d'Alene harbors some seventy million tons of lead, zinc, cadmium, arsenic, and more. Another seventy million tons lie in river bottoms upstream. All of it flows ultimately into Spokane, because suspended metals yield to hydraulic pressures and travel with currents and floods. The entire watershed could be named a Superfund site, a prospect that prompts outcries from boosters, realtors, and chambers of commerce. Cleaning up the entire Coeur d'Alene Basin—an unprecedented task, massive, as yet impossible—would involve more than twelve hundred miles of roads, yards, rivers, creeks, flood plains, Lake Coeur d'Alene, and the Spokane River.

Hoping to forestall such a job, the State of Idaho settled with some of the mining companies in 1986 for a miniscule four and a half million dollars. The Coeur d'Alene Indian tribe, which was awarded the lower one-third of Lake Coeur d'Alene in an unrelated but nonetheless high-profile lawsuit, sued the mining companies. The federal government sued two mining companies, ASARCO and Hecla, and ASARCO and Hecla countersued the federal government for its alleged responsibility in promoting metals production during World War II.

Cass Davis was one of some six hundred children whom owners of the Bunker Hill smelter sacrificed to boost profits in 1973. His brother Cal, leaded at a younger and more vulnerable age, suffers narcolepsy and has gotten by on disability assistance for many years of his life. Corinne Davis, family services coordinator for the Head Start program in the valley and mother of both boys, lived in the same house for more than thirty years. Long ago she began to work with Barbara Miller of the People's Action Coalition to redress the environmental and social injustices that have damaged her family and land.

The heaviest lead dust and zinc dust that ever fell on the Silver Valley originated in a Gulf Resources boardroom. A fire wiped out the anti-pollution filters in Gulf's "baghouse" in 1973. To fix it would necessitate a costly delay. Handwritten notes from that era estimate the number of children—laborers' kids, kids like Cass and Cal—who would get sick if production were to remain on pace. The number of would-be victims was multiplied by a per-child settlement price. Then Gulf began moving salaried employees out of danger.

Gulf Resources, owner and operator of the Bunker Hill smelter, had developed a ready liability formula that allowed it to compute such costs. The risk calculation had been easy to come by. Several years earlier, Gulf had been convicted of poisoning children in El Paso, Texas, and had had to cough up fees. And so Gulf let its Bunker Hill smelter in Idaho blast—without filters. Tons of lead rained down between September 1973 and April 1974.

The projected cost of the poisoned kids—calculated at some seven million dollars, their lives "discounted" via the science of risk analysis—proved worth it all, after a record twenty-six million dollars in profits came to roost that year. Only one family sued, the Yosses. The Yoss children were awarded precisely seven million dollars.

In 1981, Gulf shut down its legendary smelter—"Uncle Bunker," as most locals referred to it, Idaho's largest employer. The shutdown threw out of work some 2,200 employees and plunged the valley into a depression that Cass remembers well. He got free hot-lunch tickets, although sometimes he went hungry at noon instead so he could trade his lunch tickets for cash.

The depression stratified the valley, Cass says. The poor kids, the kids whose parents were out of work, the kids most disabled by toxins and least able to fend, they got ridiculed by teachers and classmates alike. Cass earned himself some punishment by "standing up for the rights of my lead-damaged friends" at Silver King Grade School in Smelterville.

Economic privation compounded illnesses and disabilities in the Silver Valley. Before people could learn how they'd been suckered by Gulf, the corporation had stashed cash in Swiss accounts and invested in trinkets offshore—a Scottish castle, some sunken treasure. Legally speaking, wrote Kathie Durbin in *The Oregonian*, Gulf's "partnership assets had been shifted through various stock and property transfers" into assets abroad.

Gulf also bilked former employees of pensions and medical benefits, a trick that Charles Hurwitz later tried to pull on workers at Kaiser Aluminum. The poverty-pocked Silver Valley became even poorer, and Gulf ran away with the embezzled funds to invest them and become the largest commercial landowner in New Zealand. U.S. corporate laws protected the scam. So did lax oversight by the Department of Justice, and a corrupt regional EPA chief whom Idaho politicians handpicked. There is plenty of blame to go around.

Such patterns of resource extraction have been repeated across the American West for more than a century. The common theme is boom and bust, cut and run. If Gulf proved expertly mobile and evasive, it also conferred mobility on the chemicals it loosed across the land. Much like land mines, chemicals such as these go on killing long after human conflicts end. The mining industry's assault on the biosphere contributes ecological repercussions for decades. Chemicals continue to migrate and pollute. Many of the workers migrate too.

For Curt "Blackie" Davis, the father of Cass and Cal, closure of the mill meant he would need to discover new ways to make a living—working on construction projects, converting railbeds to trails, nowadays selling firewood. He considers the Silver Valley home. Moving is not an option.

The Davises are acquainted with uncertainty—occupational, economic, domestic, medical, and environmental—but they have not allowed the conditions in the valley to interfere with living broad and productive lives. Their anchor-holds, amid the uncertainty, are *place* and *one another*. A boat with only one anchor roves in the wind. Two anchors hold it firm.

Chandra Gair, the married daughter and oldest child of Corinne Davis, is fortunate to have escaped the health problems that trouble her brothers. She was older when the worst lead fell. Then, too, she never rode dirt bikes in tailings piles alongside Cass and Cal. She earned a B.A. in journalism from the University of Idaho and an M.A. in Spanish from the University of Northern Iowa. When I met her she was flying a freeway to teach Spanish at North Idaho College and French at Coeur d'Alene High School. Now, a decade later, she teaches at an international school in Aberdeen, Scotland.

Chandra defends her mother's decision to continue living in the valley. A person should not remain long away from family and home, no matter what challenges. As for the pollution, she draws a shrewd analogy. "You don't move out of your house when it gets dirty," she reasons. "You clean it up." Likewise, you don't vacate if you disagree with the clean-up methods of the EPA, which she believes should broaden its program to include interior remediation.

Chandra and her husband still own an older home in Kellogg, where the dust in the furnace vent tested high in lead content. Finally she convinced the EPA to come in and clean the inside of their house. Still, she worries about other people's homes and the schools. She believes that many of her Silver Valley friends live in denial of the health hazards in their homeland.

Chandra's brother Cal, born in 1966, was the youngest in the family to endure the six-month fallout after the Bunker baghouse burned. His blood-lead levels were the highest in the family. For five years, diagnosed as narcoleptic and attention-deficit, he was on Social Security disability. Now he is working, no longer getting government benefits, but his mother says he will probably have to be on Ritalin for the rest of his life to stem his narcolepsy.

Cal Davis has been working in Alaska as a journeyman electrician. His wife Stacie and his son remain in Wallace in the valley. Stacie hopes his journeyman job works out. Cal's narcolepsy might get in the way, though, she knows, as it did in the Army when he fell asleep at attention and in chow lines. After his Army gig he was prescribed nightly downers to counteract the Ritalin that pumped him full of nervous energy and tension. Lead is known to produce "somatic problems," says Paula Lantsberger, a Spokane physician.

Cal's father Blackie coached young Golden Gloves boxers. From 1979 to 1982, Cal was Golden Gloves state champion in Idaho, Cass recalled. By seventeen, Cal had become an alcoholic, although he has been clean now for almost thirty years. Maybe he was self-medicating with booze, treating himself for lead-based afflictions that had yet to be diagnosed.

Cal's brother Cass, my old friend, worries about himself. He reaches his hands beneath the surface of the Coeur d'Alene River and comes up with a double scoop of mud mixed with lead and other heavy metals. Then he wades into the water to his thighs with sneakers and gray jeans. "I have no health insurance," he says. "I can't afford to see a doctor, and so I can never know whether my physical or mental problems are serious, normal, or related to my exposures." He thinks he is infertile, a claim the medical research supports. He also has "learning difficulties," his mother confirms, along with prostate aggravation for the past ten years. "Red meat and coffee inflame it," he says.

But most difficult of all for Cass is the periodic impotence, a state he traces to ADHD and "racing thoughts." The most desirable woman, the most interesting book—neither can hold his attention. It pains him deeply, grieves and worries him, but above all it angers him—the injustice, the uncertainty.

His acute awareness of injustice has led him to attend and spearhead protests around the Pacific Northwest against the Forest Service, against the federal agents who killed Randy Weaver's dog and wife, and against the World Trade Organization (WTO). His work as a self-employed landscaper and pond-builder does not allow him to afford the medical tests he needs to gain greater certitude.

"Shrewd business people worldwide leave a trail of polluted rivers, destroyed economies, and unclean air," Cass says. His ordeal in the Silver Valley, along with his parents' unionism, radicalized him. He joined the 1999 WTO protests in Seattle, he told me, because "Greed knows no borders." He is neither a cynic nor a defeatist, rather "an undisciplined idealist," one who "believes social change is feasible but is too lazy to reach for it," to work hard. Some activists can never do enough to satisfy themselves.

When Cass visits Pinehurst from his home in Moscow, Idaho, he notices differences in behavior, differences he attributes to people's exposures to heavy-metal mine wastes. Most of all he notices mental problems. "A lot of folks are just plain crazy," he says. "You can end up in a fistfight or worse at the drop of a hat." At school he got into fights at least once a month. His observations about his birthplace, anecdotal though they may be, again confirm what studies have shown to be a link between lead and aggressive behavior.

That link might underscore the announcement by the National Association for the Advancement of Colored People (NAACP) that it planned to sue companies that manufacture lead paint. One NAACP spokesperson called exposure to lead paint "a civil rights issue." Black children, says the group's report, are five times more likely than white people to suffer from lead poisoning. If poverty leads to lead exposure, and lead abets crime and poor health, then lead can be said to nudge indigent people toward crimes.

Nationally recognized lead expert Dr. John Rosen, head of the Children's Lead Program at the Albert Einstein College of Medicine in the Bronx, New York, believes the threshold for blood-lead in the United States—ten micrograms per deciliter—is too high. Children can be damaged, he believes, at lower concentrations. Except for the claim of narcolepsy, Rosen confirms the health allegations that the Davis brothers make.

Everyone lives downstream or downwind from someplace. Spokane and Coeur d'Alene are not only downwind from Hanford, the nuclear site that made destructive World War II bombs; they also are downstream from the Silver Valley, which ranks among the most poisoned plots of land on the planet. Mineral extraction in Idaho set free those poisons, wind and water dynamics are spreading them far, and partisan politics are delaying the cleanup.

In a three-decade flurry of concern for impacts to human health in the valley, little has been done to assess impacts to other species. Now that geologists and hydrologists are paying attention to the migration of the metals, thanks to Dr. John Osborn and the Lands Council he founded in Spokane, some stunning numbers are being recorded. Waterfowl are the hardest hit, followed by fish.

No one knows how long it will take to heal this injured watershed. Paula Lantsberger, the Spokane physician who specializes in occupational lead exposure, does not let her children swim in Lake Coeur d'Alene.

Personal testimony has a power that all the numbers in the world can't trump. Cass Davis, like a frenzied tour guide in a lower level of Hell, speaks for the damaged ecosystem he loves. He hauls up river rocks and identifies iron oxide on them. He shows slumping and blown-out hillsides below failed logging roads. He wades into the Coeur d'Alene River, from socks and shoes, to arms and shoulders, and comes up with fistfuls of lead sludge. The worst ecological damage stems from the bed-loading, he says.

Streams and rivers have beds, and those beds can be either clean or loaded by degrees. A badly loaded bed is clogged or suffocated by silt or sediment. The loaded stream and its creatures can't breathe. In the case of the Silver Valley streambeds, and now increasingly the upper Spokane River as well, the sediment from mining wastes not only makes the water toxic, but it also clogs and strangles the stream. Fish need clean beds of gravel to dig their nests and lay eggs when they spawn. Humans need clean water, too.

A first principle of ecology is that everything is connected, webbed together by invisible strands. Accordingly, the science shows, pollution from Silver Valley mines will continue migrating until the heavy logging and road-building in the upper Coeur d'Alene watershed abates.

Streambeds receive loads of sediments from roads and logged-off plots. Bare hillsides and roadways pour silted water into the river systems; they drain water that intact forests would absorb and otherwise hold. Irresponsible logging, science shows us, worsens mine wastes.

If there is plenty of blame to go around, the group that is best at evading criticism is the State of Idaho, the most conservative body

of lawmakers in the nation. Idaho leaders would like the federal government to butt out of Silver Valley affairs. Such business interests
should devolve to states and counties, to local control, they say. But
the dynamics and magnitude of the Silver Valley mining pollution are
putting that political wisdom to the test.

Corinne Davis is an educated woman, holder of an M.A. in history
from the University of Idaho. Her thesis focused on union activity in
the Silver Valley. In an odd twist of fate, she speculates, she contaminated her own yard by composting leaves and spreading the compost
on lawn and flowerbeds. She was only trying to do the right thing
for the environment. The cottonwood leaves were leaded, though,
through the roots or by means of dust in the wind, and now her lovely
landscaping and flowers must come up.

# Wrangling with Rodeo

n the northern Rockies of Washington State, Ice Age floods carved channeled scablands some fifteen thousand years ago, right at the spot where I sit with my son and wait for the Cheney Rodeo to start. The show's sponsor—U. S. Smokeless Tobacco, the owner of Copenhagen and Skoal—has emblazoned its name on all the glossy programs and the arena banners.

Reed and I perch on bleachers, whose paint is flaking from decades of hot sun. The coarse slats promise a rash if we lean back. Dressed in sandals, shorts, ball caps, and t-shirts, we feel out of place—and we are. Most everyone else wears cowboy hats. The announcer in his tower speaks as if praying for the gathered multitude. He names the United States "the greatest nation on God's green earth." Country music booms at top volume, shuddering the steel frames beneath our feet.

A radio hit by Toby Keith is playing, a militant threat of a song entitled "Courtesy of the Red, White and Blue." Its lyrics reference a roster of enemy nations. "Hey, Uncle Sam put your name at the top of his list, / and the Statue of Liberty started shaking her fist." The singer is giving a hit list, a pantheon of leaders of foreign nations soon to fall. This is a song of vengeance for the attacks on the World Trade Center and Pentagon. "Man, we lit up your world like the Fourth of July," the belligerent chorus roars. "It's gonna feel like the whole world is raining down on you, / courtesy of the Red, White and Blue!"

The sport of rodeo is kicking and very much alive in my bioregion. Ropers, riders, queens, and clowns are thrashing their limbs and stirring up dust in arena matches that pit humans against much larger mammals. This pastime, this sport, gratifies a throwback urge to subdue enormous beasts.

My son hunkers between my legs, his eyes sheltering from the sun. My hands cover his ears in a pathetic attempt to block out the heavy music that is rattling the stands. He shifts, his seat on the bleachers scratchy. It is a hot day.

Bull rider Steve Lebsack peered over his left shoulder, grimaced before a mirror, and dabbed salve on the healing wounds from a shoulder surgery. I was dressing on a bench nearby in a health club locker room in Spokane, Washington. I asked about the scars he wore. He told me all about them on that warm morning in July, the peak of the season for his favorite sport.

Steve Lebsack's afternoon and evening would be spent driving west for some seven hours, across the channeled scablands toward Puget Sound. He would rent a room and rest well, to be cocked and ready on Saturday morning for bull-riding contests in the coastal towns of Vancouver, Oakville, and Sedro Wooley. On Sunday morning he would aim his Chevy pickup back across the Columbia River, where Ice Age floods had rushed, and he would traverse the scablands to Winchester and Grangeville in the neighboring state of Idaho.

Steve weighs more than two hundred pounds, which is big for a bull rider—narrow at the hips and waist, broad-shouldered, an endomorph. When he competes, he pulls on a pink shirt and a white cowboy hat if the weather is hot, or a denim shirt and black hat for cooler days. In a fashion flourish common among thirty-something men today, he wears his hair shaved close and dyed in wispy tips up top. Beneath his tight blue jeans he favors blunt-nosed packer boots, their fringed tongues lapping, their sloping heels slung low.

In his nylon workout bag, curled from exposure to sweaty clothes, the pages of the book *Idaho's Greatest Mule Deer* confirm him as a hunter of big game. His recent shoulder surgeries would not be apt to hold him back from tramping the scabrock or competing in the rodeo ring. He is a competitor.

Healing in her own way that same day, Naomie Peasley was taking notes in an economics class at Lewis-Clark State College in Lewiston, Idaho. A member of the Colville Confederated Tribes, Naomie hails from a line of horse fanciers, arena buffs, mountain racers, and stock contractors. A former rodeo queen, dark-eyed, articulate, she was blazing a trail from the family ranch in Omak, Washington, traveling toward some form of financial independence.

A coarse ordeal laid her low in 2002. Galloping downhill in the Suicide Race during the Omak Stampede Rodeo, she fell under the hoofs of the other riders' steeds. Their hooves crushed her skull, lungs, hands, ribs. Afterward, she damn near died. En route to a hospital in Spokane, she flat-lined twice, her anxious parents sitting vigil beside her in the rescue helicopter.

"I still have flashbacks and dreams," Naomie admits. "The start of the race is signaled with a gun, and I get anxious and nervous and scared when I hear fireworks or other big bangs." Like Steve Lebsack, she plans to down a dose of rodeo again, though, once her chronic neck and backaches abate.

Aside from the rodeo, Steven and Naomie share little else. He is a bull rider, she a horse fancier and a former rodeo queen. He is European American, a slow talker with an economics degree who works as a sales representative for the Adams Tractor Company in Spokane. Naomie is still in college.

Naomie is an Indian whose great-grandfather, Leo Moomaw, founded the Omak Stampede rodeo in 1934. Naomie's dad, Larry Peasley, a stock contractor, furnishes animals to rodeos around the region. In gentlemanly dismissal of his interests, he names it his "expensive hobby." On his ranch, his daughter came of age under the spell of horseflesh, and she still rides horses every chance she gets. The Peasleys strive to accommodate rodeo's growing commercialization and keep the sport alive. They integrate Anglo and Native cultures when they do, defining fit roles for women in a male-centered sport.

Inside the thousands of sanctioned Western rodeos every year, gender lines are evident. Rodeo queens and their courts heighten awareness of the sport in public appearances. They strive to be eye-catching in tight blouses and high-domed hats. They take charge of enhancing rodeo's image, glamorizing it a bit; they also aim to shift the controversial emphasis away from the animals. They ride and preside in barrel races and grand entries.

Wardrobes for national rodeo queens (never use the word *costume*) can cost fifteen thousand dollars. While men like Steve Lebsack do most of the riding and roping, wear the biggest belt buckles and hats, the women who orbit them, dubbed "buckle bunnies" by unkind pundits, prove useful for dressing and undressing wounds. Other women, like Naomie Peasley, never seem content just to flutter, flatter, and adorn the scene.

The queen and her princesses kick off the Cheney Rodeo. Reed is wide-eyed and bored at the same time. In the women's wild breakout they race around the arena, whip the necks of the horses, and spurt dirt from their hooves. All six women wear leather chaps (said with an *sh-* sound) adorned in glitter, fringes, and calfskin bleached and dyed in red, white, and blue.

Reed and I still are suffering from the heat, the itchy bleacher seats, the noise, and the dust. On the heels of the breakout the grand entry begins, where the women parade to display "the greatest flag of all, the flag we call Old Glory." The announcer in his tower invokes the flag in tones as low as though he were mourning. The national anthem solemnizes us all. Those who wear cowboy hats doff them, becoming suddenly as humble as beheaded flowers.

The show is underway. "Wolffy" the clown starts making his rounds, goofing in sneakers and suspenders and oversized bloomers. Scaling fences and leaping, he returns catcalls and flirts with the girls. He has a microphone so everyone gets privy to his wit. The announcer chuckles and dubs him "a guy who wears makeup. You must be from California, the land of fruits and nuts."

The rapid prattle from these microphones is lost on my son. Attending his first rodeo, he is fidgeting, glancing at my watch. A chute opens. A lasso yanks a calf off its feet and slams it down. Laughter bubbles from the crowd.

Outside the laughter, the grounds of rodeo are under siege. People for the Ethical Treatment of Animals (PETA), in a volley in this culture war, has built a website it dubs "Buck the Rodeo." The site features half-clad actress Bonnie-Jill Laflin, tousled, grumpy, lying alone in a pile of hay. This advertising campaign is captioned by the sentiment, "No one likes an eight-second ride."

Rodeo fans, though, defend the eight-second ride and their right to view it and do it. Placed on the defensive, they claim that rodeo enhances family values, brings together relatives and friends, and builds self-esteem that may endure a lifetime. To frustrate animal advocates who might blight the wholesome fun of rodeo, an industry-supported front group, the Animal Welfare Council (AWC), aims to cut such advocates off at the pass. The AWC works to "support the use of animals in recreation, entertainment and sport."

For rural economies that historically depended on natural resources, rodeo carries the status of custom and culture. It hearkens back to a time when most of the skills on display in rodeo arenas had application on a ranch. Rodeo filters out political ambiguities and the challenges of urban lives.

Rodeo also turns a profit, thanks to corporate sponsorships, a large following, and recent coverage by the mass media, including ESPN and *Sports Illustrated*. Chambers of commerce long have boosted rodeo as homegrown entertainment that can prove useful for marketing local wares. Reed and I are seated in an arena that host auctions, car shows, and monster truck rallies in the off-season. Local auto dealers wheel their wares into this stadium as well.

Rodeo is an extreme sport. It includes events like bull riding, bareback bronc riding, saddle bronc riding, bulldogging (aka steer wrestling), steer roping, calf roping, team roping, barrel racing, and more. Steers for wrestling can weigh half a ton, while bulls bred for riding in the rodeo can run a full ton.

These creatures possess intelligence and complex emotions that often prove seductive to cowboys. Just as some girls find bad boys hard to resist, cowboys often gravitate toward volatile beasts. Other extreme sports entail the manipulation of inanimate objects, such as kayaks or bikes, carabiners or skis, but muscular bulls and horses fight back against rough handling, all the more so when flank straps and electric prods make their moods rank.

Stockmen look for bulls and broncs that are resistant, tough, willing to buck. These are known as the rank trophy animals. The tight-cinched flank strap may function to agitate the animal's groin. The rider holds a chest rope in one hand and flails the air with the other. Before the chute opens, the animal may also legally receive an electric jolt to persuade it to perform. After the chute opens, a game of strength and wits ensues. Rider and mount each strive to outlast the other, making roughstock events akin to hunting—a competition to the death—and to athletic sex.

Several days a week, Steve Lebsack can be found in the gym shaping up for the bulls. He lifts weights and runs, taking extra time to stretch. Already in his early thirties, his remaining days as a competitor are few. "I'm old for this game," he confesses, saying he'll give it up after one more year. A belated fan of rodeo, he admires both Brant Collier, thirty, and former bull-riding champion Rob Sweeney, thirty-six, now retired and owner of a Spokane-area construction firm. Standing alongside them, Steve feels as if he's "barely fit to carry their lunch." He was disappointed not to have made the roster to ride the bulls in the Cheney Rodeo this year, a consequence of his low yearly earnings.

If hero exaltation contributes to this pastime, there is also reverence for the animals, akin to the respect some hunters extend toward their prey. Success for riders depends on which animal is chosen in the case of racers, or which one is drawn in the case of buckaroos. Officials select the names of particular animals to pair with competitors in roughstock events. Points get awarded for the animal's difficulty, for the rider's technique, and for keeping one hand always in the air. A thrashing arm might get "stretched out" during a rough ride, the announcer at the Cheney Rodeo quipped.

A rank bull or bronc earns a rider a higher score, but every ride has to last a full eight seconds to earn any points at all. Steve Lebsack sustained his worst injuries on Slingshot, and a note of veneration still creeps into his voice when he names that bull. Maybe Slingshot had been "eating too much gunpowder," another gag in the patter that pours from announcers' boxes.

Shoulder injuries are common among bull riders, but less fortunate riders also suffer head or face injuries, making hockey helmets more common now. Collier got "whipped down," slammed by a bull's skull, so he now carries metal in his head. Lebsack wears two plates and twelve screws in his left arm, and four plates and ten screws in his face. One wonders if patched-up cowboys set off metal detectors in airports.

Rodeo is a young man's sport. It is also a game played mostly by single men. Many wives and girlfriends would object to such rigorous routines. When the Cheney Rodeo began on July 9, 2005, Lebsack was flying to Oregon to ride in Cottage Grove, Sweet Home, and places in between.

Frank "Bo" Campbell, a government major at Eastern Washington University, rode bulls when he was in his teens and twenties. At fifty-two, he looked back fondly on his rodeoing when he was seventeen years old and 140 pounds. Bo was so into the sport that he moved to Oklahoma in 1970 to study under Freckles Brown, the legendary bull rider. Said to have broken every bone in his body, Freckles remained competitive into his fifties.

Bo eventually wised up, retired from the rodeo long ago. He was one of my better students. More interested in philosophy and politics than in rodeo now, more concerned about U.S. foreign policy than bulls, Bo would not have favored the patriotic hoo-hah at the Cheney Rodeo. I don't ask him about it, though, for fear I'll come off as a crank, a citified critic looking for some smut.

"In 1970, I landed funny on my shoulder in Libby and dislocated it," Bo recalled. Physicians in that Montana town were weary of patching up busted cowboys. A dislocation sometimes had to fix itself. "They would load you up with morphine, then sit back and wait till it came back." His physician, rushed or impatient, wrenched some ligaments in Bo's shoulder. Bo's injury grew worse. "Later my opposite side got strong and pulled my back out of whack, so my spine curved." Finally Bo had surgery, and now a big scar encircles the rotator cuff on his shoulder. Asked how rodeo animals were treated, he replied, "Some contractors took better care than others. Some kept animals in hot pens, with barely adequate water and feed, trucking them a long ways."

In the Omak Stampede, the event in which Naomie hit the dust, fifteen or twenty Suicide Race riders whoop their steeds down a 225-foot grade of sixty-two degrees, swim the Okanogan River, scramble up a dirt ramp, and sprint a hundred yards to the finish line. Since 1983, at least eighteen horses have died in the race, just as Naomie almost did in 2002.

Dr. Jim Gjesvold, Omak Stampede board member and veterinarian, scoffs at a newspaper reporter's suggestion that rodeo animals are abused. The Suicide Race is safer than flat-track horse racing, he claims. Both PETA and the Progressive Animal Welfare Society (PAWS) dispute him. PAWS calls it "the deadliest horse race in North America," and in 2004 three horses died in the three days of the race. A guarded Gjesvold says, "No horse worth taking down that hill could be forced down the hill. Like the riders, they love to do it."

Gjesvold's comment brings to mind a sweetheart from long ago. Her nostrils flared like an Arab mare's when she was at her most intense. Fresh from a stressful marriage and a Vietnam veteran husband who had abused her for years, she admitted in a moment of intimacy and sad candor that she felt as if she needed to be injured just to trust that she was loved.

The first North American rodeos took place in Mexico. The Spanish for "cowboy," *vaquero*, comes from cow, *vaca*. Vaqueros roped horses, bulls, anything that moved—even grizzly bears, now extinct throughout the region. Those grizzlies must have thought they had ascended into heaven when the slow elk—an old joke throughout the Pacific Northwest—began to low among them. Rather than rope their cows on roundups, vaqueros pursued and hamstrung them with sharp, curved knives. By 1888, rodeos spread to the United States and Canada by way of Indian reservations and reserves.

For the pleasure of paying customers, Buffalo Bill's Wild West shaped those proto-rodeos. Its extravaganza is hard to calculate today. It featured reenactments of bison hunts, attacks on helpless settlers' cabins, Custer's Last Stand. Many of the dramatized scenes, like the scalping of settlers, were grisly. All were patriotic. (Historically known as "the unkindest cut," scalping did not definitely originate with the Indians. Its evolution is still a subject of debate.) In 1887, Buffalo Bill Cody's pageant toured Europe to grand huzzahs.

Stateside, William Cody earned his name in the same way he earned his pay—an early railway corporation awarded him a dollar-sixty-seven for every bison he shot. A one-month salary penciled out to some three hundred bison slain. The 1976 Robert Altman film about him, *Buffalo Bill and the Indians, or Sitting Bull's History Lesson*, stars Paul Newman as the alcoholic Cody, being flattered by impresario Ned Salsbury played by Joel Grey.

Mexican horsemen were the first buckaroos, in the multiculturalism that colored early rodeos. The Wild West of Cody showcased Indians like Sitting Bull as objects both of ridicule and wonder. In a competing show, Geronimo, from the back seat of a car, made a spectacle of blasting captive bison, whose meat his employers barbecued and served on platters to visiting dignitaries. African American cowboy

Bill Pickett, the Dusky Demon from Texas, as his employer advertised him, invented the sport of bulldogging. At only five-foot-seven and 145 pounds, Pickett leapt from the backs of galloping horses, tackled fleeing steers, grabbed their horns, wrenched their necks, and bit their upper lips until they gave in.

Today's rules forbid rodeo contestants to bite steers. Animal welfare groups won a 1913 battle to outlaw the bite-'em technique that Pickett had learned from crossbred Texas bulldogs that clamped on the lips of cattle to bring them to their knees. In England, Pickett upset animal rights advocates, who felt that twisting necks was "horrible steer torture." English police arrested him in 1914 and fined him twenty-five dollars. His boss coughed up the fine, week after week, considering it a fair-enough trade for all the lush publicity. And so the show went on.

Control of nature was in Bill Pickett's blood, as it must be in every rodeo contestant to a greater or lesser degree. While Bill was trying to lasso a wild coyote in 1928, his horse stepped in a hole, flipped, and broke its neck. Unable to pull himself free, he lay beneath the dead horse for an hour.

Early rodeos held particular values for Indians. Animals, known within some tribes as the "Ones Without Fires," harbor powers withheld from human beings, and particular tribes attributed their own gift powers to horses. A sprinting horse moved like a god across the ground. Rodeo enhanced the skills needed in raiding, which offered the means to increase horse herds. Then, too, wild horses had to be tamed, subdued, and broken before they could be ridden. Broken horses had to be taught to turn, stop, and accelerate on command. Rodeos in those days honed such practical skills. Bull riding never has had practical application in ranch work, though. It is pure show, and even so it always proves to be the show that draws the biggest crowds and cues the rowdiest songs. We spectators thrive on the promise of violence.

Many rodeo events evolved in Indian communities, and so it proved to be a biting irony when certain early rodeos barred Indian competitors. High entry fees and long travel times thwarted them as well. They suspected some non-Indian judges harbored prejudices or grudges, awarding them low scores in the competitions, depriving them of rightful prizes. In the pageantry that made up rodeo, until recent decades, Natives were consigned to stereotypical roles—mugging in sham encampments, wearing fake headdresses, and mock-scalping humble sodbusters. Demeaned by such roles, Indians formed their own groups, like the All Indian Professional Rodeo Cowboys Association, and their own rodeo events, like the Suicide Race in Omak, Washington.

Hundreds of all-Indian rodeos take place every year in the United States and Canada and help maintain traditional ties, much like pow-wows do. Annual rodeos become ritual occasions for whites and Indians alike. Families and friends return from soft jobs far away, gather and swap stories, compare injuries and awards. An abiding sense of place grows stronger, ancient ties with animals too, in ways that may infuriate activists for animal rights.

European Americans and Natives today are facing more and more protest when they enforce perceptions that they are using animals for needless food or callous sport. The Makah Indian tribe's harpoon hunt for gray whales is only one of the high profile battles in culture wars being waged over nature around the American West. In 1999, Makah hunters in Washington state killed a whale and now display its skeleton in a tribal museum in Neah Bay, an act that divided Seattle-area watchers and even some members of their own tribe. My blacksmith buddy Darryl Nelson admires their pluck, though. "If they want to water-ski behind a fifty-foot whale," he said of those Makah hunters, "let 'em have at it."

Western civilization long has followed laws that safeguard animals from harm. Americans may not beat or starve or mutilate a domestic animal without threat of legal reprisal today, may not drive motor vehicles into wilderness areas since the passage of the Wilderness Act of 1964, may not "harvest" or otherwise take threatened creatures since Richard Nixon signed the Endangered Species Act in 1973. Such laws, designed to protect nature, also extend it particular rights. We depend on nature, the argument goes, and when we harm other species or ecosystems we jeopardize ourselves. Children exposed to animal cruelty may be damaged by that exposure, in the most extreme of cases devolving into serial murderers like Ted Bundy and Jeffrey Dahmer, who began their forays into sadism with animal abuse.

Organizations like the Illinois-based Showing Animals Respect and Kindness (SHARK) are arranging boycotts of corporations that sponsor rodeo. SHARK's "tiger video" truck features four program-mable LED signs. Its mammoth video screens, one of them a full hundred inches high, project images of rodeo abuse and its members sometimes patrol outside rodeo grounds.

When Indian riders or hunters find their traditional practices op-posed by animal activists, a ticklish mix of ideologies can arise. There are so very few Americans who seem to side with the animal advo-cates, though, that fur-farm saboteurs and eco-saboteurs have resided for years at the top of intelligence community lists of domestic terror-ists. Such semantic sleight of hand mysteriously associates liberators of factory-farmed foxes and minks with Middle East "suiciders," as George W. Bush named Islamic bombers in a speech defending his administration's War on Terror.

Naomie Peasely always liked to vie against the guys. Growing up rid-ing horses on the steep hillsides of her Omak ranch, she practiced ro-deo skills with bluster. She also got hurt. "I had a couple of emergency room visits. Just look at my face." The marks she pointed to looked like acne pocks. "Those scars are from trying to cut off a group of horses and turn them towards home, but running into a thick tree and brush wall instead." Twigs were protruding from her cheeks that day, she said, and blood was running down her face. "Yeah, after that epi-sode they called me 'The Woman from Snowy River.' I've also been called 'Crazy Bitch' because nobody seems to be able to keep up with our bucking horses in a rocky, cliff-like pasture except me."

Basketball cemented and legitimized her drive to compete brutally. "I have been playing since I was about in the second grade. I also played soccer, baseball, tetherball, and other activities on the play-ground that I could beat all the boys at." She'd always dubbed herself a tomboy, so it must have come as some surprise to her family when she chose to run for Okanogan County Junior Queen at the age of nine, then for Nespelem Junior Rodeo Queen at sixteen. She won both runs. At nineteen she rode in the Suicide Race. At the age of twenty-two, finishing her degree to become a high-school English teacher, she was still attending rodeos, but only as a spectator and fan.

Fitting into the mold of a rodeo queen was easy for her. "I had to fix my hair. Speak properly. Smile a lot. Sit up straight with my legs crossed; I think this was the hardest thing to remember. Back home

I was the same old me. I beat up the boys and sat like one too." She had to show skills with a horse, deliver a speech, answer impromptu questions, and appear in "fancy western wear, tucked in, yes. I had a crown and a sash I had to wear in public. I had to ride in parades and go to luncheons." And she had to compete.

For the book *Rodeo Queens and the American Dream*, Joan Burbick interviewed women who were queens from the 1940s through the 1990s. In the early decades, the rodeo queens were more apt to be appointed than to be named winners. Boosters aiming to rally rodeo's flagging fame manipulated them, some queens believed. Other queens saw rodeo as an opportunity to advance economically and socially. All the former queens had photo albums they cherished, as Peasley herself still does, and several displayed portraits of themselves in full regalia hanging on their living room walls.

Peasley is proud of her family's traditional footing in rodeo. When she walks, she looks as if she's setting out to kick some serious ass. "My Uncle Don, who has passed away, was a Tribal Council member. My Aunt Patty runs a logging company and has been a secretary or judge of the Omak Stampede and Suicide Race for many years. My granddad, Ed Peasley, was a well-known horse trainer, trader, and breeder." Like the writer Sherman Alexie, who grew up in the Spokane Tribe not very far away, her voice itself possesses a strut.

Having come of age in a town known more for rodeo than for any of its splendid natural features, she sees little difference between Indians and whites as competitors, and in fact she insists that rodeo as an institution has afforded her an uncommon seat at the table. "It is not really a matter of race. Rodeo is a culture in itself. If you rodeo, you are part of a whole community." That rodeo culture entails a swagger. She characterizes the body language of the swagger as saying, "Hey, I'm tougher and more talented than you."

Endurance racing is deeply embedded in the culture of the Colvilles, whose large reservation covers nearly one and a half million acres of wild, rugged lands. Naomie had grown up with many of the former Suicide Race champions, and was sure she could succeed against them. "Women had competed in the past," she said. "Either they were in the back of the pack or they ended up where I did, the hospital." Even so, she set out to put her proud American boast beside the guys.

The president of the 2002 Omak Stampede, the late "Cactus" Jack

Miller, said Naomie was leading the pack of riders down the steep hill to the river until she fell at the water's edge. The horse she rode, Black Charlie, had won the race before, but he might have been too hot for her to handle. As he was "setting up" before plunging in the river, Black Charlie slowed so fast he ejected Peasley, who had been leading and was whipping hard with one hand to increase her speed. She takes full responsibility for the crash. Miller listed her injuries as a fractured skull, a broken hand, and an injured rib. The leader of the pack, she ended up being trampled by it.

In the helicopter bound for Sacred Heart Hospital in Spokane, she was having seizures and ceasing to breathe. Her scalp had a laceration six inches long, and she was losing blood. Her lungs had to be pumped to remove river water she inhaled when she fell, and one lung collapsed in the process. For a year afterward, she needed the care of a neurologist.

Her brain was wounded, too. "I didn't know how to deal with it, turned to alcohol, became depressed for months." Cognitive problems compound her emotional distress. "Names and numbers are still hard for me, when before I never had a problem. This may sound weird, but I had to learn how to remember all over again."

The news media were conspicuously absent in the coverage of her ordeal—as if reporters or editors were too nervous to take on the story. Had they taken it on, they would have risked darkening the already dark cloud that has been gathering over the Suicide Race since it began in 1935, three years after the Omak Stampede itself kicked off. No one seems to want to call such a cherished cultural tradition into question. In that respect, the blind eye is entirely American: better to ignore the controversy than tell anyone about it.

One year after her wreck—after she made the nearly fatal mistake of wrangling with one of the toughest events in all of rodeo— Naomie Peasley returned to the course as a spectator. When she got there "all the emotions came flooding back" to her. Some quivering part of her wanted to be in that race again. Another part wanted "to escape, to run away, to grab every one of those guys by the throat and ask them, 'What the hell are you thinking?'"

A trial-by-fire tranquility invests her. When she loosed the floodwaters of that event, I could see a kind of distance in her eyes. Her hair was black, her figure fit, her voice one of confidence and awe. It was hard to shake the feeling that she was speaking as a person who had trudged back from the dead. A prophet in long black braids, she alone had escaped to tell the world the truth.

I was tempted to ask how her parents would respond to the prospect of her return to the race as a competitor. Would they support her as they did before? Buy her clothes, help her train, frame her photos, and cheer her on?

Rodeo is in the eye of a storm. As many people and animals as it kills every year, it continues to enjoy canonical status throughout America. It appeals most to those who are homesick for the stark simplicities of the Old West. By 1959, forty-eight Western shows had been produced for prime-time television. DVDs and TV shows still cater to fans of *Gunsmoke*, *Maverick*, *Bonanza*, and *The Rifleman*.

In the novel *Fencing the Sky*, by James Galvin, a character yearns for "the other world, the world before this world, the way of life that promised never to end and then ended." If fans insist that rodeo enhances family values, it is hard to pick a fight with parents who find roping and riding preferable to fast food, drugs, and motorized recreation. Rodeo is the lesser of several evils.

In the days of edifying family entertainment, chautauquas originated in an upstate New York town by the same name. Chautauquas proved, for several decades, to be popular outlets for roving educators and entertainers, much like the radio show *Prairie Home Companion* does today. Still today, chautauquas have much in common with the rodeos that supplanted them. Both arose in late nineteenth-century America. Both take place in dedicated spaces. Rodeo's space, known as the arena, remains idle for most of the year, yielding only to occasional tractor pulls, monster truck rallies, demolition derbies, and dirt-bike races.

Rodeos, like chautauquas, fuse music, dramatic performances, and public lectures. The music of rodeo is invariably country. Its dramatics come from clowns in makeup and baggy pants, from rodeo queens in tight jeans and sparkling tiaras and colorful chaps, and from human and animal athletes locked in contests that can end in injury or death. Rodeo's public lectures issue from homey and wisecracking announcers who offer moral and political guidance under entertainment's guise. Like chautauquas also, rodeos occur during the summer, in outdoor settings, as part of a set circuit. A contestant's circuit may include six rodeos in a weekend, over three or more days, several states, and a thousand miles. Audiences like Reed and me support them.

Instead of educating in the way of the liberal arts, instead of offering intellectual views, rodeos build their esprit de corps by making appeals to patriotism, conservative values, and to the control of nature. Rodeo is a rural diversion, a stunted chautauqua where human athletes wrangle with animals in a kind of barnyard drag. Spurs, spangles, boots, chaps, jeans, hats, and big-buckled belts are as stylized as stockings and high heels. Formulaic in its trappings, rodeo sells a standardized product, a set of ritual gestures and moves that find their way into mainstream culture through music videos, wardrobes, and advertising. Rodeo embodies a desire for escape to a prior and simpler time, when values seemed to range closer to some comfortable absolute, when the shock of the modern had yet to impart scars.

Part of rodeo's appeal is that it addresses a conflicted yearning for a bygone time. It tries to satisfy an imperialist nostalgia. Many European Americans romanticize the same cultures their ancestors tried to destroy, said anthropologist Renato Rosaldo, who didn't directly consider the mass-culture phenomenon of rodeo in his book. Such romanticizing allows immigrants to cope with the neo-colonial guilt that comes from being the beneficiaries of centuries of conquest. Many rodeo fans share family roots in rural landscapes, a legacy that grew out of Manifest Destiny, and Rosaldo's definition of imperialism applies well to the various territorial imperatives that complicate American culture. "The peculiarity of their yearning," he wrote of nostalgia-mongers, is that they "long for the very forms of life they intentionally altered or destroyed."

One function of the cowboy boot was to guard against snakebite, but the tables have turned. In an ad for cowboy boots that ran in magazines when I was young, an image of a rattlesnake pinioned beneath a boot heel was used to market the very boot that subdues it. In the ad, a hand reaches down with a big blade to behead the hapless snake. "People mourn the passing of what they themselves have transformed," Rosaldo notes, with a gentle simplicity.

It bewilders, the process of yearning for what one has destroyed, but rodeo as a cultural category had to be invented. "During the last decade of the nineteenth century," Rosaldo reminds us, "as the frontier was closing, racism was codified and people began to deify nature and its Native American inhabitants." A century later, the frontier has long been closed, but rodeo remains a forceful demonstration that the frontier's sense of wildness and rank possibility may still be summoned. One need only pay an admission fee — twelve to twenty-four dollars — to recapture a sense of the past.

The quest to subdue animals, if only for the eight seconds of a ride on a bucking bronco or pinwheeling bull, confirms the rodeo contestant in his more elevated identity. The quest bestows upon him the powers of those mighty beasts. Just as the successful hunter may come to associate with his prey, so does the rodeo rider. The master of the bull borrows traits from the bull, just as the rider of the racehorse takes upon herself the fleetness of her steed. Few people have the capacity, Rosaldo notes, both to "yearn for the old ways and acknowledge their warrior role in destroying them." We yearn well.

Today in North America, when the non-animal Cirque du Soleil has a broader following than the other circuses do, rodeo still draws big audiences. Supporters claim it is the most popular spectator sport on the continent, surpassing football in the United States and hockey in Canada for the number of paying watchers it annually draws. The leisure and liberty implicit in rodeo have come to be associated with Texas, the adoptive home of George W. Bush, and imperialist nostalgia may explain support for both those institutions.

Finishing up the Cheney Rodeo, Reed and I stray past the bleachers to find him some late lunch. At every food stand the smoke curls up, grilled and barbecued meat, a food he will not eat. Reed settles on fry bread, doughy pastry on a paper plate. We buy it from an Indian who is overweight and sweating. Grease speckles his thick lenses. The fry bread is yummy, Reed says, crisp on the outside, soft within, drizzled with honey, loaded with carbs.

It is just what Reed needs after our ordeal of a drive through the channeled scablands, an afternoon spent in the hot sun, and the blitz of stimuli from speakers mounted high on poles around the grounds. He has seen rodeo animals ridden, roped, panting, jerked, and spurred. He has watched the clouds of dust rise from their fun.

# Technologies of Doubt

This story of Pacific Northwest salmon can be told the economic way: how some farmers and paper workers, jet-boat operators and port commissioners, reliant on Snake River waters stilled by dams, fear their livelihoods are being ravaged by rising beliefs that some dams must be breached.

Or it can be told the scientific way: how a vast majority of American biologists have concurred—and petitioned presidents and Congress to confirm—that breaching or bypassing the four lower dams on the Snake River in Washington and Idaho is necessary to recover the wild salmon.

Or the story can be told culturally: how American Indians have filled their physical and spiritual needs for thousands of years, speared and netted salmon guaranteed by nineteenth-century treaties, and shared with European Americans the river's bounty for more than two hundred years.

You will hear the story told many ways in the Pacific Northwest, although rarely in the same social circles. Across the wide political divide, there is little middle ground. Ever since the Army Corps of Engineers conducted hearings around the region to gauge sentiment about the salmon, questions of whether to breach dams are appearing on the radar screens of politicians everywhere.

Before I tell these opposing stories, I should tell the salmon story in more personal terms: how I grew up as a witness to a culture war and never knew it, as a resident of a state that resides in the eye of the storm over salmon recovery, but above all I would tell how, as a believer in a powerful technology, I came to be assured it could save the fish.

During my lifetime, faith has become a habit. Not the faith of orga-
nized religion, rather faith in technology. I have faith my car will start
when I go to work. And if my car breaks, I have faith that mechanics
can repair it so I can drive it back to work to earn the money to pay
for those repairs. As a child I learned, along with the rest of postwar America, to believe in engineers, whether those engineers worked
with NASA, with Chevrolet, or with the Army Corps when they proposed to build Wanapum Dam on the Columbia River near Mattawa,
Washington.

As a Washington native, I traveled to a riverside town near Mattawa with my parents to fish, camp, and hunt. Before the Wanapum
Dam flooded the land, we discovered sage grouse, black widow spiders, and Native American pictographs. Water covered that magi-
cal landscape. My sadness diminished through my belief in technical
leaders, economists, and politicians who said the dam was necessary
to generate electricity and control floods.

When the fish runs began to decline, doubt briefly touched my
faith. Maybe building the dams was wrong. But I drowned my doubt
and learned new stories. The engineers guaranteed they had a plan.
They would retrofit the Columbia dams with fish ladders to aid the
upstream struggle of the fish.

Later I learned that those hundreds of miles of slack-water reservoirs created by the dams took a lethal toll on the young fish heading
downstream to the ocean. The salmon smolts lose velocity, they lose
time, they grow old before they reach the sea, they become victims of
predatory pike-minnows that thrive in that slack water, and they can
die from nitrogen saturation when they plunge over the spillways of
the dams. But the engineers and politicians had an answer to those
problems, too. Pack the fish in barges and take them around the dams
and slack water, they decreed. And so it came to be. Never mind the
absurdity of the image: hundreds of tons of steel toting tiny minnows
past millions of tons of concrete that had been built up in their way.

I tried to push aside the illogic of a second technology being invented to "remediate" a first technology, a knotty process that required a newer and longer verb to supplant the old-school verb "rem-
edy." When the managers of game fish kicked off the pike-minnow
bounty program, I thought it was good. I caught a few pike-minnows
myself. Some people tried to make a living by bounty fishing, like in

the Old West. Maybe, just maybe, a new sport fishery would offset the loss of hundreds of thousands of salmon and steelhead.

I remember those salmon running in the Green, Cedar, Skagit, and Skykomish rivers of western Washington, spawning in gravel beds, thrashing on stream banks, others in other rivers traveling as much as nine hundred miles up twisting routes into Idaho and Montana.

When we dredged the silt held back by dams and made islands where terns nested and ate the smolts, I believed it right to be manipulating nature that way. Reason urged me to doubt, but faith stood in my way.

Now I am growing older and more numb. I've heard the promises come and watched the fish runs go. It's getting harder to believe. To remediate one problem, the technologically savvy Army Corps proposed covering the silt islands they had built with plastic, planting bushes to deter the terns, or building new and better islands out of harm's way, outside the ancient salmon path.

These are solutions I once might have praised. But my faith in the technical specialists in Spokane, Walla Walla, Olympia, and Washington, D.C., has diminished along with the salmon runs. Today when Idaho senators, the *Seattle Times*, and the regional chambers of commerce of cities around me continue to support the dams, when partisan interests predict that parts of eastern Washington will revert to sagebrush and desert if we abandon the dams, when they argue that electricity rates will shoot through the roof and that we simply cannot afford to save the salmon, I no longer believe them. In the Tri-Cities of Richland, Pasco, and Kennewick, Washington state's elected officials rally for the dams with vehemence usually reserved for "the children," or for "democracy." They choose economic subsidies over the region's most majestic and—until now, the most enduring—natural resource.

And even though my trust in the experts has been shattered, I can't quite break the habit. I still have a grain of faith that the Army Corps will make the right decision when it comes out with yet another technological fix to save the salmon. A federal judge is requiring them to do so. There is one plan on the table that the politicized Army Corps is loath to suggest, a plan that might work. The engineers could bypass the same dams they built, giving the river back its current to let wild salmon run free again.

The lower Snake River flows 140 miles from Lewiston, Idaho, to the river's confluence with the Columbia. The largest branch of the Columbia, the Snake used to produce more Chinook, sockeye, and steelhead than any tributary in the basin. A million fish used to migrate hundreds of meandering miles to tiny streams and lakes containing spawning grounds deep inside Idaho and Montana every year. Redfish Lake, high in Idaho's Sawtooth Mountains, takes its name from the color of its exhausted spawners.

Between Lewiston in Idaho and Pasco in Washington, the Army Corps built four controversial dams between 1962 and 1975 — Ice Harbor, Lower Monumental, Little Goose, and Lower Granite. Those dams stanched the river's flow, turning its swift current into slackwater reservoirs that hastened the pace of commercial exchange in the barging of paper and grain. Biologists at the Idaho Department of Fish and Game have said for years that breaching those four dams is crucial to saving Snake River salmon.

Fish runs on the Columbia and Snake rivers have plummeted from some sixteen million adults returning to spawn per year to fewer than one million now. Of that million, four-fifths begin life in hatcheries. The number of wild fish left — a genetic wake-up call — is incalculably small. Thirteen runs of salmon and steelhead on these rivers are classed as legally endangered today. Authority over the fish is fragmented among the governments of seven Western states and British Columbia, nine federal agencies, and thirteen sovereign Indian tribes.

Technological fixes have cost billions of dollars. Some of those fixes include collecting fish with giant screens, loading them in trucks and barges, moving them downriver around the dams, curtailing predatory seals in Puget Sound, killing marauding sea lions below the dams, and curbing farmers far inland who plow too close to the water's edge or use tons of chemical inputs.

Despite these great efforts, paid for by taxpayers, the fish continue to decline. The dozens of concrete dams remain. Those who fear dam breaching, though, claim that other factors — terns, commercial net fishermen, El Niño — are more responsible than dams for the steep population declines.

Breaching dams means removing the earthen portion alongside the concrete dam face. Such removal means the water then sweeps past the dam, and later the earth may be restored, if need be. This process does not require destruction of the dam, simply a bypass of it.

One valid objection to breaching is the question of what will become of the millions of tons of silt that have piled up behind the dams over so many years. Rivers naturally carry silt and dump it in the process of flooding. That dumping used to enrich the soil. Now it just piles up. And so the Army Corps has been dredging and constructing artificial islands to dispose of the silt.

The loss of salmon is dire in economic terms alone. Commercial and sport fishing towns on the Washington coast—Westport, Neah Bay, Seiku—flicker at a fraction of their former glory. Protecting dams and dispossessing fishermen will cause the United States to break treaties with Canada and Pacific Northwest tribes. Those tribes alone could prove eligible for thirteen billion dollars in compensation for the fishing rights guaranteed by a treaty made in 1855.

Now the feud between business interests and champions of dam breaching is forcing the region's reluctant leaders to take sides. Washington's recent governors—all of them criticized by dam fans for being too soft—are more committed in their opposition to the Snake River dams. Three-term senator Slade Gorton, who swore that dams would not be breached on his watch, lost his job to a political novice, Maria Cantwell, who is friendlier to the environment. Oregon's recent governors have consistently supported dam breaching. A series of governors in neighboring Idaho, meanwhile, have argued time and again that breaching the dams is no way to save salmon.

Would-be presidents on the campaign trail in this millennium have enlivened the debate. Senator Bill Bradley, during a visit to Seattle as part of the 2000 election season, made clear he would not rule out the possibility of breaching. "I'd have to get a full report at the time," he said. "I'd ultimately have the final decision, but what I want to do is involve the states much more in the process." Senator John McCain spoke likewise. "I would leave it on the table," he said. "I wouldn't rule it out, no." George W. Bush set himself apart from his opponents when he spoke against breaching in the dam-friendly Tri-Cities a week before the presidential contest he won. The administration of Barack Obama has maintained the status quo on the matter of the dams.

Whether and how to restore the salmon has become a battleground in the American culture wars over the environment. Former Oregon governor John Kitzhaber strongly supported dam breaching in an address to the American Fisheries Society. Alaska Governor Tony Knowles, later replaced by the less fish-friendly Sarah Palin, characterized the Snake River dams as "a killing field," deadly especially for Alaska's fish-dependent economy. And in Oregon, federal judge Jim Redden has sent both the Bush and Obama administrations back to the drawing board to build more sound science into their biological opinions, which he found inadequate for restoring the flagging fish runs.

Elsewhere there seems to be growing support for salmon. The City Council of Astoria, Oregon, voted unanimously to urge the federal government to remove the dams. Tom Udall, a Democrat in New Mexico, became the first member of Congress publicly to endorse breaching the four Snake River dams. Taxpayers for Common Sense ranked the Snake River dams among the most wasteful projects in the United States and criticized the Army Corps as "out of control." Salmon fans in the Pacific Northwest agree.

The history of dams and salmon is saturated in irony. We Americans, or at least our ancestors, believed technology could preserve migratory fish. And so we took fish for granted, treated them as harvestable commodities, squandered them as fertilizer, and erected concrete barricades in their way. Such ironies deepened with passage of the Endangered Species Act (ESA) of 1973, signed into law by President Richard Nixon, a Republican whose party now generally condemns the act as an impediment to pro-growth mandates. One of the environmental movement's most cranky apologists, Edward Abbey, reminded Americans that "growth for growth's sake is the ideology of the cancer cell."

A quarter-century before the passage of the Endangered Species Act, Shirley Hoehn grew up in the eastern Washington town of Beverly, near Mattawa, where Crab Creek flows into the Columbia River. She remembers the fish runs firsthand. She blames "government folly" for the loss of various sub-species of silver, sockeye, and Chinook salmon. She saw the fish cluster so thick that her mother, "standing in waist-deep water, was almost drowned by a school of salmon. Dad ran in to help her out of the fish."

The shallow meandering of Crab Creek makes it prone to flood. After McNary Dam was completed in 1956—justified by arguments for flood control—Shirley noted that the dam "merely moved floods back into the tributaries and relocated them. The Columbia River flood in 1947 was at my front door, and I know the only thing floods hurt is human convenience. For nature there is nothing more beneficial than a flood." Flood control has never been an issue or a benefit, though, in developing and defending the lower Snake River dams.

Shirley Hoehn criticizes environmentalists as "Johnny-come-latelys" who have little sense of history. "For seven years I lived right on the Columbia River and saw firsthand the greed and stupidity that created all those dams, wrongly designed, lacking foresight and all regard for the perpetual life cycles necessary to sustain healthy land and water." She wonders why it took people so long to see the proverbial handwriting about salmon on the wall. She finds it no surprise that dams are destroying the greatest fish runs in the lower forty-eight states.

Shirley counters the belief that hydroelectric projects incidentally killed them. Rather, Shirley asserts, the government understood that salmon would become extinct due to the dams. When McNary Dam was under construction, salmon so often clogged the site they forced workers to "stop to clear out the fish—again and again and again. So Washington State said, 'Let's get rid of the fish.' And they did in 1948 and 1949." Some laborers actually bulldozed the salmon clutter into piles. Photos of that activity are impossible to find.

A mere sixty years ago, before hydroelectricity projects and farms began carving the upper Columbia River bioregion, young Shirley found joy in sharing her life with "pygmy rabbits, cougars, bobcats, diamondbacks," and other useless or intrusive species that brought character to her home. Each spring she grew delighted by "purple sage in bloom, phlox, larkspur, blue bells, yellow bells, and delicious wild onions." Her rueful regard for reclamation projects on the Columbia tributaries proves to be an exception to the all-too-human rule.

Among opponents of dam breaching, the most vocal have been the pulp and paper workers for Clearwater Paper Corporation. As the largest employer in Lewiston, Idaho, a town 465 miles inland, Clearwater benefits hugely from the slack water behind the dams. Thanks to slack water, Clearwater is able to float forest products (wood chips) to its factory and finished products (paper and paper pulp) to major markets downstream. Thanks to more than one hundred million dollars in yearly subsidies to operate the barges, reservoirs, and dams, the Clearwater mill remains viable despite a flood of cheap Canadian goods.

Frank Carroll, communications director for Clearwater, laments that there is no assurance that breaching will rescue salmon. He yearns for certainty. He asserts in the newspaper *High Country News* that no one yet has "made the case conclusively that dam breaching will bring the fish back, or that other actions can't also do the job." He asks for proof. He wants more consideration also for the custom and culture that the dams have come to afford him.

Carroll comes from a line of people who relied on the Mississippi River for a living. He speaks of an "ongoing federal/private partnership" that has made it feasible for people to "reclaim Eden from the wilderness," referencing the Bureau of Reclamation, to improve nature and extract a handsome living from its resources. "The burden of salmon recovery," he reasons, "shouldn't be heaped only on the shoulders of those who have come to rely on the dams."

Frank Carroll suggests that the cultural claims of Native Americans are neither viable nor apt today. He evokes an Indian acquaintance that wants to see American bison restored, who hearkens to "1855, the sacred year when his treaty was signed. There were sixteen million fish coming home then. Maybe there were sixteen million buffalo then. Things were different then." In other words, we can't turn back the clock. And yet in western water law, legal scholars have shown, appropriation claims go by the rule of "first in time, first in right."

Mr. Carroll says his beleaguered community compares to "the Balkans, where people, focused on surviving gunfire, never give a moment's thought to matters of the environment. Remember the last news story you heard about endangered species conservation in Bosnia?" His comparison suggests that Americans need to lay off his region and people to cultivate a renewed sensitivity for the environment and an appreciation for its needs.

A member of the Colville Tribe, Leroy Eadie hails from the Lake band. His people used the "huge salmon runs" on the Wenatchee River as a main food source and as a trading product. By the time Eadie was coming of age, during the 1970s, his people "mostly ate deer meat and food commodities: powdered eggs, canned potatoes, blocks of American cheese." Salmon had grown rare by then, only "served at Indian dances, weddings, or other special events. There is a lot of spiritual meaning in food, in how it is consumed and what order." Today he is the director of parks for the city of Spokane, where he tries to do right by the environmental ethics he inherited from his family and tribe.

Salmon have slid from the center to the side of Eadie's family's lives. "My uncle would bring salmon from further south on the river, or we would go and catch some at the Chief Joseph dam. We'd throw big three-prong hooks into the water and snag them." That dam, named with no apparent irony after an Indian leader who fled federal troops in Oregon, halted the salmon and caused them to "just hang out there confused by the cement barrier. My brother still travels there, but I can't bring myself to stand on the concrete, snag, and drag the fish up walls. I fish now on the reservation for brook trout."

The dams are a sore subject for Leroy Eadie. He wants to see them breached—as he has said at multiple hearings sponsored by the Army Corps. At one of those hearings, he "talked about [his] grandfather teaching [them] to offer thanks to both the creator and to the animal who gave its life for [their] consumption." Thinking about the vanished salmon and about his late grandfather, Mose Cleveland, was difficult for him. "I wondered what he would suggest we say as a culture when we took an entire species. At that point it has gone way beyond thanks."

The onslaught leveled at the salmon goes against the native grain of honoring the dead. Grabbing habitat from the fish, killing them by degrees, violates the teachings of Leroy's grandfather. "He taught us to not let an animal suffer. Kill the animal quickly and give your thanks. It is much more of an emotional connection to the circle of life when you look a dead animal in the eye and thank it for giving its life for you." Maybe his family and cultural practices suggest what ought to be done to the remaining salmon in the Snake River: conciliate them, propitiate them, if we can't save them.

Speaking without emotion about breaching the dams, Eadie concedes, "some of the economic impact arguments are legit." Just as breaching the dams might harm factories and farms, though, he reminds us that dams historically "wiped out the local Indian economy. I think some economic aid is in order—maybe federal, maybe state, maybe Bill Gates. Resolve the economic impact issue and breaching becomes even more of a no-brainer." Eadie shares the belief of the vast majority of citizens testifying at Army Corps hearings around the region—that breaching is an easy call.

The Spokane Area Chamber of Commerce, though, has vocally opposed breaching the dams. In public hearings around the region, the Chamber has taken an activist approach on behalf of its eighteen hundred member organizations. In a survey of those organizations, "seventy-six percent of those responding supported maintaining all of the existing uses of the river system, and only ten percent were opposed." The key phrase might be "of those responding." Those people who have an economic stake in "the existing uses of the river" would certainly be most apt to respond, just as those who routinely vote in elections would be most apt to cling to an inherited faith in the fairness of politics.

The Chamber sponsored a "summit" entitled "Breaching the Dams: At What Cost." The meeting featured only anti-breaching interests. Slade Gorton, at that time a Republican senator for Washington State, attended the event. "The purpose of the summit," according to Public Affairs Director Dan Kirschner of the Chamber, "was to provide a counterpoint to all of the media attention being focused on the emotional option of breaching the dams." .

Adopting a mantra common in business, Kirschner believes that we can have it all, strong growth and a sound environment, even when local economies continue to extract natural resources. "The Chamber supports salmon recovery that doesn't force the region into a false choice between people and fish, between livelihoods and salmon life-cycles. This country has the resources and the expertise available to accommodate both." The current economic downturn has hardened his adherents further. Members of the Chamber's member organizations express worry that government will "force" them to abide by a ruinous "false choice."

If the Spokane Chamber wielded a legal scepter, our society would rescind or modify the Endangered Species Act—the regulation that requires the salmon be saved. "The inflexibility of the ESA," Kirschner believes, "has led to its abuse by many groups and individuals who continue to use the current law as a weapon against industries in the Inland Northwest and elsewhere." Laws certainly are being used defensively to protect ecosystem health and human health. Like Frank Carroll in Lewiston, Kirschner's language suggests he and his clients feel under assault or siege.

The Spokane Chamber "supports amending the ESA to provide for more flexible and realistic regulations that consider and provide options for mitigating the economic impacts of recovery actions." So does Rep. Cathy McMorris Rodgers, who has held hearings around the region to assess the temper of her constituents regarding the tensions between economic interests and the ESA. The ESA is a scapegoat for weak economies. What a travesty it would be if industrialists, politicians, and chambers of commerce were to use cyclically poor economies to support the legal evisceration of the ESA.

In whom should the public place its trust, as it decides how to restore the salmon runs under ESA guidelines? One proof test in natural-resource matters is to follow the money trail. To pose it as a question, who stands to profit most in dollars and cents from policy decisions?

Not environmental organizations, those nonprofits whose grants and memberships fall off with good news. They will not profit materially from dam breaching. Possibly Indians, whose treaty rights have been abrogated by dams. But their historical losses are more cultural than economic, and they stand to lose a great legal investment if any suit should prove unsuccessful.

Following the money trail leads to some of the least sustainable of the industries in the Pacific Northwest and the northern Rockies. The money trail leads to agribusinesses, notorious for creating record erosion rates and topsoil that blows and flows into the rivers and the sea, for plowing to every hilltop and creek bottom, and for torching wheat stubble and bluegrass and damning the consequences for public health.

Following the money trail leads also to Georgia-Pacific, the Clearwater Corporation and other timber interests, to groups that cut forests on public lands — old-growth timber when they can get it, ancient conifers to be chipped and cooked into paper products, bleached with chlorine that washes into the watershed, into Puget Sound, the Clearwater River, the Snake River, and the Columbia River. Clearwater has a permit to discharge forty million gallons of its heated effluent into the Snake River at Lewiston every day. In another irony of history, Clearwater is named for a tributary of the Snake River that flows past it, a river now made warmer and turbid by its industrial discharges.

As the salmon cycle gasps its last breath, the economic cycle continues. Those organizations most implicated in the degradation of salmon habitats are also most vigorously engaged in denying scientific facts, dodging legal obligations, and opposing social change. Now that they have the counter-scientific machinery in place, it is an easy move to deny global climate change.

My flagging faith in technology has become a crisis. Hundreds of hours spent keyboarding, piloting cars down highways, and watching projections on screens make me ache to lie down within earshot of water. Occasionally I do. If I am lucky the water will be booming, caddis flies hatching in the shallows, wild geese trading cries, and big trout rising or rolling below the falls.

# Acknowledgments

Grateful acknowledgment is made to the editors of these journals for first publishing the following essays: "Genius Loci" in *Sewanee Review*; "High Country" in *Brevity*; "In the Shadow of the Government's Blind Eye" in *Organization and Environment*, published by Sage/Society Publications, http://online.sagepub.com; "Magpie in the Window" in *Memoir (and)*; "Under the Sign of Aries" in *North Dakota Quarterly*; and "Walker Creek" (originally published as "Living the Land") in *Weber Studies*.

My thanks to Eastern Washington University and its Northwest Institute for Advanced Study for three summer indulgences, during which time many of these essays were written; appreciation especially for support, editorial and otherwise, from EWU colleagues Sam Ligon, Dana Elder, and Larry Kiser. Also I wish to thank John Balaban, Michael Branch, Mary Clearman Blew, Annie Dillard, Michael Frome, Christopher Howell, Derrick Jensen, John Keeble, William Kittredge, Natalie Kusz, Carrie Lipe, Kathleen Dean Moore, Annie Oakes, Robert Michael Pyle, Pattiann Rogers, Sharman Apt Russell, and Gary Snyder—who helped in ways they might not even know. Finally, to my wife and children, for the gifts of time they gave unstintingly.

## sightline books
*The Iowa Series in Literary Nonfiction*